MW00453013

Aquarienpflanzen ▪ Plantes Aquatiques ▪ Onderwaterlandschappen

# Aquarium Plants

## The Practical Guide

## By Pablo Tepoot

**new life
publications**

AQUARIUM PLANTS:
THE PRACTICAL GUIDE.
European Edition
Copyright © 1998 by New Life Publications,
A Subsidiary of New Life Exotic Fish, Inc.

All rights reserved. No part of this book may be
reproduced or utilized in any form or by any means,
electronic or mechanical, including photocopying,
recording by any information storage and retrieval
system, without permission in writing from the
publisher. Inquiries should be addressed to New Life
Publications, 25855 S.W. 193 Ave. Homestead, Fl.
33031.

Published by:
**New Life Publications**
25855 S.W. 193 Ave.
Homestead, Fl. 33031
Tel: (305)245-2404
Fax: (305) 248-7450


ISBN 0-9645058-4-3


Printed in Hong Kong.

# Aquarium Plants

## The Practical Guide

**Photographs:**
Pablo Tepoot

**Written by:**
Pablo Tepoot

**Book Design & Production:**
Ian M. Tepoot

**Book Organization:**
Ian M. Tepoot

**Editors (English):**
Judy Leiby
Ian M. Tepoot

**Translation & Editing (German):**
Beate T. Lindsey

**Translation (French & Dutch):**
International Aquarium Tech of Belgium

**Editing (French & Dutch):**
Reginal Popelier

*Photographs: C. striolata, C. sulpurea, C. amicorum, C. glaseri, C. siamensis by Robert Gasser.

**new life publications**

# Acknowledgments

*Dedicated to James Thiele of Naranja Aquatic Nursery,
for the generous time dedicated to this project.*

Most of the plants pictured in this book were provided by *Bruce McLane* and *Brad McLane*, Florida Aquatic Nursery. Without their help, creating this volume would have been impossible. Some plants were provided by *James Thiele*.

Our gratitude to *Dr. Leo Morin*, Seachem Labs, for checking the accuracy of the chemistry in the Introduction to Aquarium Plants section of the book. In addition, thanks to *Guy Oei*, who provided insight into aquarium plants in the shop setting.

Finally, thank you to *Reginald Popelier*, of International Aquarium Tech of Belgium, for helping to verify some of the plant names used in this book.

Finally, *Ian Tepoot's* design and typesetting made it possible to produce this book. Ian was awarded first and second place in the nationwide Logo Design Competition (1994 & 1995 respectively) sponsored by the Association for Education in Journalism and Mass Communication (an international association of college professors). He was also chosen for the 1998 prestigious Dean's Cup for Professional Promise - an award from the School of Journalism, University of Florida, U.S.A.

According to Elaine Wagner, professor of advertising, University of Florida: "Ian is very talented and dedicated to quality design and production work....I respect his knowledge of computers and his talent as a designer."

# Notes on Names

The scientific names provided in this book conform to the standard form for scientific naming. The following is an explanation of the naming system used in this book:

- All described species are described using the genus name followed by the species, both in italics. The genus name is begun with a capital, the species name is noted in all lowercase letters.

    **Example:** *Genus species*

- Undescribed species whose genus is known are written using the convention: genus (in italics) followed by "sp." and a common or trade name surrounded by quotes.

    **Example:** *Genus* sp. "Name"

- Various varieties of a species are noted with "v." followed by the variety name.

    **Example:** *Genus species* v. "Variety Name"

- Hybrids are indicated by the symbol "x." followed by a variety name. This convention is generally applied to domestic or man-made varieties.

    **Example:** genus species x. "Variety"

# Foreword

The aquarium hobby is progressing through the most exciting period of time in its history! It is only fitting that a book of this caliber is now released. Today, there are numerous varieties of plants available and they are readily accessible. Because of the improved products and advanced techniques available, keeping aquatic plants has never been easier. Through this brilliant, unparalleled photography, hands-on experience, and detailed research, the author is able to present—in easy to read terms—this well organized and knowledgeable book of aquarium plants. Armed with the information contained in this book, anyone can become an accomplished plant aquarist.

The variety of aquarium plants in this book reflects what is available today. Many new varieties have resulted from growers' interest in sport selection and hybridization. Some examples of sport selection are the colorful *Hyrophila polysperma* "Tropic Sunset" and the unusually shaped *Microsorium pteropus* "Windelov." Hybridization has introduced such spectacular plants as *Echinodorus* "Ozelot" and Echinodorus "Rose." The cloning of plants through tissue culture has increased the availability of plants that were notoriously slow propagators. Plants such as *Anubias coffeefolia* and *Echinodorus* "Rubin" are now easy to obtain by the hobbyist at reasonable prices.

Due to the greater interest in aquarium plants, manufacturers have produced more sophisticated products than ever before, making aquatic plant keeping easy. Metal halide lights and $CO_2$ injectors, although more expensive, are now commonplace. The correct choice of light, coupled with proper nutrition, will cause your plants to flourish. The author explains in simple terms, exactly how to set up your tank to accomplish the lush plant growth documented photographically in the following pages. If you follow the author's formula, you also will be able to grow plants as beautiful as those seen in this book. The dark age of plastic plants is a thing of the past!

Speciation of aquatic plants has been in a state of constant change for years. Many of the names cited in this book may be different from those your are accustomed to. I attempted to use the most recent literature available, as well as personal communication with experts in the field, such as Robert Gasser and Jim Thiele. In some cases, it was not possible to speciate a plant, so rather than list a possible incorrect name, I stopped with genera.

With the large selection of plants displayed in this book, how will you ever choose the right plants for your aquarium? The author simplifies this process by categorizing plants into three main groups; true aquatic, terrarium, and floating. These categories should help the novice aquarist choose the right type of plant for his particular need. It is our hope that by categorizing plants in such a way, the novice will not be discouraged by buying a terrarium plant and watching it die, only to believe he was the cause of its demise. On the contrary, armed with this book, a novice will have a rewarding aquatic gardening experience.

– Brad McLane

# Contents

# Preface

*In the kingdom of the blind, the man with one eye is king.* I think that saying perfectly captures the reason I wrote *Aquarium Plants: The Practical Guide*. I believe that when it comes to keeping a beautiful planted aquarium, many of us are living in the "kingdom of the blind."

I hear from many hobbyists here in the United States who claim that they don't use any special techniques in caring for their aquarium plants (for example, they use only standard aquarium lights and undergravel filters), and yet their plants are beautiful and healthy. My response to such claims is this book. The mediocre vegetation we see in our tanks seems acceptable often only because we have seen little better to compare it with.

In the section *Comparing Methods*, you will see photos of a plant that I raised outside in sunlight (in a continuous water flow and with a group of swordtails), using none of the plantkeeping techniques discussed in this book. I then placed the same plant in an aquarium that had been setup according to the principles in this book. You can judge the results for yourself.

All of this brings me back to one of my main purposes in creating this book: to provide hobbyists with information about *practical* and *proven* methods for keeping a beautiful planted aquarium. Occasionally, even without proper care, your plants *may* (and I emphasize *may*) thrive beautifully. But armed with the proper knowledge, anyone can keep beautiful aquarium plants *reliably.*

As of 1997, hobbyists in Europe and Asia are admittedly ahead of us in the art of keeping beautiful planted aquariums. However, I have faith that we U.S. hobbyists can produce planted aquariums as wondrous as those found in any other country *if* we acknowledge the deficiencies in the state of the art as it is currently practiced within the United States.

The hobby of keeping coral reef tanks is a good example of an area in which we have made great strides forward in knowledge and techniques. In the early 1970s, most marine aquarists used bleached coral and inefficient under-gravel filters in their tank systems. But thanks to such modern equipment as wet/dry filters, chiller, protein skimmers, and U.V. lights, maintaining a coral reef tank is much more feasible today. We need to make similar progress in maintaining aquarium plants; actually, this transition from older methods to more modern methods should be easier with plants than it was with coral. One driving force behind this book is to promote the use of effective, proven methods.

Of course, like all the books produced by New Life Publications, *Aquarium Plants: The Practical Guide* is also designed to be a reliable reference guide to a wide range of aquarium plant varieties. Each plant included in the book is illustrated with a beautiful and — more importantly — *true-to-life* photos that are the trademark of our books.

Not only does filling the book with gorgeous photos of *natural* plants in beautiful condition allow us to provide a reliable reference guide, it also serves to highlight the deficiencies of plastic plants. I believe hobbyists tend to use fake plants because they often do not have the information they need to keep natural plants healthy, so their plants become sickly looking and seem to be difficult to maintain. That's a situation I hope this book remedies. By providing simple guidelines for keeping beautiful plants and by providing pictures that show the full splendor of real plants, I hope to convince hobbyists that their is no reason for them to choose plastic plants over real plants. Let's face it; no matter how good quality a plastic plant is, it still looks *plastic*. Furthermore, plastic plants cannot perform photosynthesis (which helps oxygenate the water) or help neutralize nitrogenous waste. Real plants can provide these functions, which can reduce the occurrence of "new tank syndrome." This syndrome is the tendency for there to be high mortality rates among the fish placed in newly settup aquariums. By placing plants in an aquarium before adding the fish, you can go a long way toward "conditioning" the environment for the fish. Also, throughout their lives, fish tend to do better in tanks containing real plants than in tanks with a "plastic environment."

Another issue *Aquarium Plants: The Practical Guide* addresses is the mistaken use of bog -plants, terrarium plants, and other non-aquatic plants in aquariums. By providing a reference on true aquarium plants, I hope to educate consumers on which plants will thrive in a submerged, aquarium environment. In addition, included in this book is a section on non-aquarium plants that serves as a sort of "what to avoid" list. This section has photos for reference so that hobbyists can avoid them on sight.

Why do non-aquarium plants remain popular with aquarists? These plants invariably die underwater, and so many beautiful aquarium plants are available! I sincerely believe that the mortality is so high for all plants that people simply *do not notice* that these non-aquarium varieties cannot be maintained. If aquatic plants can be kept more effectively, people will lose the "cut flower" mentality so prevalent among aquarium plant hobbyists. Cut flowers may look fine, but they die quickly.

*Aquarium Plants: The Practical Guide* is our fourth book, and the philosophy we followed in producing this book is the same one we followed in producing all our other books: to create unique and beautiful books that are both art and powerful reference tools.

Another common thread connecting all our books is our focus on *clarity* and *simplicity*. I believe books can be scientifically accurate and informative without sacrificing clarity. In fact, to be a powerful reference, I am convinced that a book must be easy to understand. It does not matter how much data is stuffed into a book if it is not clear and easy to use. Toward this end, all the entries in the *Aquarium Plants* section of this book have an information bar that presents vital information on keeping each variety in an at-a-glance format. Fans of our other books may recognize the information bar from our *Marine Aquarium Companion*. This icon-and text-based summary for each variety was so well-received that it will likely be a consistent feature of all our reference works.

A theme we keep stressing in all our books is that simply having a lot of text should not be a goal in itself. In fact, just the opposite is true. Readers should be able to get the most possible information with the least amount of text. Many readers have a "term paper" mentality in which the *quantity* of text becomes more important than the *quality* of the data provided. Our books contain densely packed and *practical* information in the simplest possible format. Various pieces of information in this book were carefully screened for accuracy. Brad McLean of Florida Aquatic Nursery (the largest U.S. aquarium plant producer) verified the data for the entries on each variety. Dr. Leo Morin of Seachem Labs, Inc. examined much of this books information regarding water chemistry.

We hope that this book will be a valuable resource for you in the set up, maintenance, and selection of aquarium plants. But (just as important) we hope that *Aquarium Plants: The Practical Guide* will provide many hours of enjoyment.

# Vorwort

*Aquariumpflanzen: Ein praktischer Leitfaden* (*Aquarium Plants: The Practical Guide*) ist das vierte Buch von New Life Publications, und das erste Buch, in dem wir die Welt bepflanzter Aquarien erforschen. Dieses Thema paßt gut zu unseren anderen Büchern, d.h. unseren Büchern mit den Titeln *Cichliden: Ein Bildband*. Pflanzen sind ein lebenswichtiger Bestandteil jedes gesunden Ökosystems eines Aquariums. Die Fische sind für die Pflanzen von Nutzen — und umgekehrt; dies ist ein Beispiel für die hervorragenden wechselseitigen Beziehungen in der Natur.

Natürlich kann man in einem Aquarium kein vollständiges Ökosystem einrichten, das dem Ökosystem in der Natur entsprechen würde. Es gibt jedoch Methoden, mit denen Ihr Aquarium gedeihen kann. All dies bringt mich zu dem Hauptzweck dieses Buches zurück: ich möchte Hobby-Aquarianern Informationen über *praktische* und *bewährte* Methoden geben, anhand derer sie sich ein wunderschönes bepflanztes Aquarium einrichten können. Wenn man mit den richtigen Kenntnissen bewaffnet ist, kann sich jedermann *zuverlässig* wunderschöne Aquariumpflanzen halten.

Der Abschnitt *Methodenvergleich* enthält Fotos einer Pflanze, die ich im Freien (in ständig strömendem Wasser und mit einer Gruppe von Schwertschwänzen) in der Sonne gezüchtet habe, und hierbei keine der Methoden für die Pflanzenpflege verwendet habe, die in diesem Buch angesprochen werden. Ich habe diese Pflanze dann in ein Aquarium gesetzt, das nach den Prinzipien in diesem Buch eingerichtet wurde. Sie können selber sehen, welche Resultate dies hatte.

Man konnte 1997 sehen, daß Hobby-Aquarianer in Europa und Asien die Kunst, sich ein wunderschönes bepflanztes Aquarium zu halten, sehr gut gemeistert haben. Hobby-Aquarianer in den USA sind zwar in der Pflege von Aquariumpflanzen nicht so versiert, machen aber jedes Jahr Fortschritte. Ich bin der Meinung, daß Hobby-Aquarianer in den USA (vielleicht mit Hilfe dieses Buchs) innerhalb von ein paar Jahren bepflanzte Aquarien produzieren werden, die genauso wundersam wie Aquarien in anderen Ländern sind.

Korallenriff-Aquarien sind ein gutes Beispiel dafür, auf welchem Gebiet Hobby-Aquarianer rund um die Welt große Fortschritte hinsichtlich Wissen und Techniken gemacht haben. Anfang der siebziger Jahre haben die meisten Meeresaquarianer gebleichte Korallen und ineffiziente Filter unter dem Kies in ihren Aquarien verwendet. Aber dank moderner Geräte wie Naß-/Trockenfiltern, Kühlvorrichtungen, Proteinabschöpfern und UV-Lampen ist die Haltung eines Korallenriff-Aquariums heute viel einfacher. Wir müssen bei der Haltung von Aquariumpflanzen ähnliche Fortschritte erzielen; und der Übergang von älteren Methoden zu moderneren Methoden dürfte mit Pflanzen einfacher als mit Korallen sein. Eine treibende Kraft hinter diesem Buch ist, die Verwendung effektiver und bewährter Methoden zu fördern.

Natürlich ist *Aquariumpflanzen: Ein praktischer Leitfaden* genau wie alle anderen Bücher von New Life Publications darauf ausgerichtet, ein zuverlässiges Nachschlagewerk für ein großes Sortiment an verschiedenen Sorten von Aquariumpflanzen zu bieten. Jede Pflanze in diesem Buch ist in wunderschönen und — was noch wichtiger ist — lebensechten Fotos zu sehen, die das Wahrzeichen unserer Bücher sind.

Dadurch, daß wird das Buch mit Fotos von Naturpflanzen in wunderschönem Zustand gefüllt haben, konnten wir nicht nur ein zuverlässiges Nachschlagewerk zusammenstellen, sondern gleichzeitig auch die Mängel von Plastikpflanzen hervorheben. Ich glaube, Hobby-Aquarianer verwenden künstliche Pflanzen hauptsächlich aus einem Grund: wenn sie nicht über die Informationen verfügen, die sie benötigen, damit ihre Pflanzen in einem gutem Zustand bleiben, scheinen Plastikpflanzen eine einfache Lösung zu sein. Dies ist eine Situation, die mit diesem Buch hoffentlich beseitigt wird. Ich hoffe, daß ich Hobby-Aquarianer mit einfachen Richtlinien, die dazu beitragen, daß die Pflanzen schön bleiben, und mit den Fotos, auf denen die ganze Pracht echter Pflanzen zu sehen ist, davon überzeugen kann, daß es keinen Grund gibt, Plastikpflanzen echten Pflanzen vorzuziehen. Wir wissen

doch alle, daß eine Plastikpflanze ungeachtet dessen, wie gut ihre Qualität ist, trotzdem noch wie *Plastik* aussieht. Darüber hinaus können Plastikpflanzen keine Photosynthese ausführen (die dabei hilft, das Wasser mit Sauerstoff anzureichern) oder dabei helfen, stickstoffhaltige Abfälle zu neutralisieren. Echte Pflanzen können diese Funktionen liefern, wodurch das „Syndrom neues Aquarium" weniger oft auftritt. Bei diesem Syndrom handelt es sich darum, daß unter Fischen, die in ein neu eingerichtet Aquarium gesetzt werden, eine große Sterblichkeitsrate herrscht. Wenn Sie Pflanzen in Ihr Aquarium setzen, bevor Sie Fische hinzufügen, können Sie die Umgebung für die Fische „aufbereiten." Außerdem gedeihen Fische in Aquarien, die echte Pflanzen enthalten, ihr ganzes Leben lang besser als in Aquarien mit einer „Plastikumgebung."

Ein weiteres Thema, das in *Aquariumpflanzen: Ein praktischer Leitfaden* angesprochen wird, ist die falsche Verwendung von Moorpflanzen, Terrariumpflanzen und anderen, nicht-aquatischen Pflanzen in Aquarien. Ich hoffe, daß ich die Verbraucher mit diesem Nachschlagewerk über echte Aquariumpflanzen darüber aufklären kann, welche Pflanzen unter Wasser in einer Aquariumsumgebung gedeihen werden. Außerdem enthält dieses Buch einen Abschnitt über Pflanzen, die nicht für Aquarien geeignet sind und dient als eine Art „was Sie vermeiden sollten"-Liste. Dieser Abschnitt enthält ebenfalls Fotos, damit Hobby-Aquarianer diese Pflanzen auf den ersten Blick vermeiden können.

New Life Publications hat sich wie immer das Ziel gesetzt, Informationen zu liefern, mit denen Hobby-Aquarianer ermuntert werden, weil die Kunst der Einrichtung und Pflege eines Aquariums so deutlich und zuverlässig wie möglich erklärt wird. Wir sind bei der Produktion von *Aquariumpflanzen: Ein praktischer Leitfaden* der gleichen Philosophie wie bei allen unseren anderen Büchern gefolgt: wir wollen einzigartige und wunderschöne Bücher verfassen, die sowohl Kunst als auch überzeugende Nachschlagewerke sind.

Ein Nachweis für unsere Philosophie ist unsere Konzentration auf *Klarheit* und *Schlichtheit*. Ich bin der Meinung, Bücher können wissenschaftlich exakt und informativ sein, ohne daß die Klarheit leidet. Tatsächlich bin ich davon überzeugt, daß ein Buch einfach zu verstehen sein muß, damit es ein wirkungsvolles Nachschlagewerk ist. Es ist egal, wie viele Daten in ein Buch gestopft werden, so lange es nicht klar und einfach zu benutzen ist. In diesem Sinne haben alle Einträge im Abschnitt *Aquariumpflanzen* einen Informationsbalken, der auf einen Blick wichtige Informationen über die Haltung jeder Sorte bietet. Fans unserer Bücher erkennen den Informationsbalken eventuell aus unserem *Marine Aquarium Companion* wieder. Diese auf Symbolen und Text basierende Zusammenfassung für jede Sorte hat soviel Anklang gefunden, daß sie in Zukunft höchstwahrscheinlich in allen unseren Nachschlagewerken zu finden sein wird.

Wir betonen in allen unseren Büchern, daß es kein Ziel sein sollte, einfach nur eine Menge Text zu haben. Genau das Gegenteil stimmt. Der Leser sollte in der Lage sein, mit der geringsten Menge an Text so viel Informationen wie möglich zu erhalten. Viele Leser haben eine „Studienarbeit"- Mentalität, bei der die *Quantität* des Texts wichtiger als die *Qualität* der Daten ist, die abgeliefert werden. Unsere Bücher sind mit *praktischen* Informationen im schlichtesten Format vollgepackt.

Eine Reihe von Informationen in diesem Buch wurden sorgfältig auf ihre Genauigkeit untersucht. Brad Maclean von der Florida Aquatic Nursery (der größten Produzentin von Aquariumpflanzen in den USA) hat die Daten in den Einträgen für jede Pflanzenart überprüft. Dr. Leo Morin von Seachem Labs, Inc. hat einen großen Teil der Informationen über die Wasserchemie in diesem Buch untersucht.

Wir hoffen, daß Ihnen dieses Buch bei der Einrichtung, Pflege und Auswahl Ihrer Aquariumpflanzen als ein wertvolles Nachschlagewerk dienen wird. Aber (was genauso wichtig ist) wir hoffen auch, daß Ihnen *Aquariumpflanzen: Ein praktischer Leitfaden* viele vergnügliche Stunden bereiten wird.

# Préface

*Aquarium plants: The Practical Guide* est le quatrième livre publié par "New Life Publications" et le premier explorant le monde des plantes d'aquarium. Il fait suite à la série sur les cichlidés appelée: *Cichlids: The Pictorial Guide*.

Les plantes sont un élément prépondérant dans l'écosystème d'un aquarium. Les poissons ont besoin des plantes, mais l'inverse est vrai aussi. Cette relation est un exemple des liens interactifs existant dans la nature.

Bien entendu, on ne peut pas installer dans un aquarium un écosystème correspondant totalement à ce que l'on trouve dans la nature. Toutefois, il y a des méthodes permettant de garder un aquarium en belle forme. Cette constatation est une des motivations qui m'ont poussées à écrire un livre, un guide apportant aux hobbyistes des informations pratiques et éprouvées sur la façon de maintenir un aquarium avec de belles plantes. Vous constaterez qu'armé des conseils adaptés n'importe qui peut conserver de belles plantes d'aquarium.

Dans la partie "les méthodes comparées," vous verrez les photos d'une plante que j'ai laissée dehors exposée à la lumière du soleil (dans un flot continu d'eau et avec un groupe de *Xyphos*). Je n'ai utilisé aucune méthode décrite dans ce livre. Je plaçai ensuite la même plante dans un aquarium en suivant les principes de l'ouvrage. Vous jugerez vous même du résultat.

Depuis 1997, les hobbyistes européens et asiatiques ont fait de belles choses dans le domaine de la maintenance de beaux aquariums plantés. Les hobbyistes américains, même s'ils n'ont pas encore atteint leur niveau, progressent très rapidement. Je pense qu'en quelques années (peut-être que ce livre y contribuera!) les hobbyistes américains parviendront à élever des plantes aussi magnifiques que celles que l'on trouve dans les autres pays.

Un bon exemple de la progression des techniques et des connaissances grâce à l'engagement des hobbyistes est le domaine des invertébrés. Dans les années 70, la plupart des aquariophiles utilisaient des coraux blanchis et des filtres sous sable à l'efficacité douteuse dans leurs aquariums d'eau de mer. Mais grâce aux nouvelles techniques telles que les filtres secs-humides, les écumeurs, les groupes-froid, les stérilisateurs UV etc…la maintenance d'invertébrés et de coraux en aquarium n'est plus impossible. Nous avons besoin d'avancer de la même façon dans le domaine des plantes.

En réalité, le passage aux techniques nouvelles devrait être plus facile dans le domaine des plantes que dans le domaine de l'eau de mer. Ainsi, ce livre se donne pour but de promouvoir les procédés les plus actuels qui ont fait leur preuves.

Bien entendu, comme tous les ouvrages publiés par New Life Publications, *Aquarium plants: The practical guide* prend le chemin de devenir une référence fiable, guidant le lecteur à travers la grande variété des plantes aquatiques. Chaque plante du livre est illustrée par de magnifiques photos qui font la renommée de nos ouvrages.

Il ne suffit pas de montrer des photos de belles plantes en bonne santé pour se présenter comme guide de référence. Cet ouvrage vous informera également des déficiences provoquées par les plantes en plastique. Je pense que les hobbyistes ont tendance à utiliser de fausses plantes pour une simple raison: le manque d'informations. On comprendra que lorsque l'on ne sait pas maintenir de vraies plantes, on préfère en prendre des fausses. En leur prodiguant les conseils dont ils ont besoin, je tenterai de convaincre ces hobbyistes

de la beauté des vraies plantes et d'infléchir leur choix vers la véritable plante aquatique. De toutes les façons, la plus belle plante en plastique donnera toujours une impression de plastique.

D'autre part, elle ne produira pas de photosynthèse (ce qui est primordial pour la vie d'un aquarium en oxygènant l'eau par exemple) ou ne participera pas à la neutralisation de certains déchets azotés. Les vrais plantes ont ces fonctions et peuvent réduire "le syndrome de l'eau neuve" qui se manifeste par une forte mortalité de poissons lors de l'installation de l'aquarium. Ainsi, en mettant des plantes dans l'aquarium quelques jours avant de mettre les poissons, on contribue à préparer l'eau et à la rendre viable pour les poissons. De même, les poissons se comporteront mieux dans un aquarium planté avec de véritablesplantes qu'avec des plantes en plastique.

Un autre problème soulevé par *Aquarium plants: The practical guide* concerne l'introduction de plantes de marais ou de terrarium dans l'aquarium. Le fait de donner une référence sur les véritables plantes aquatiques peut éduquer le lecteur et l'aider à effectuer le bon choix pour éviter une mortalité importante par l'emploi de plantes non immergeables.

D'autre part, un autre chapitre concerne les plantes non-aquatiques qu'il faut absolument éviter de placer dans un aquarium. Grâce à cette liste illustrée par des photos, le lecteur pourra les reconnaître facilement.

Comme toujours, l'objectif de New Life Publications est de fournir les informations qui encouragent le lecteur à installer un aquarium et à le maintenir dans de bonnes conditions. La philosophie suivie pour la publication de cet ouvrage reste la même que pour les autres livres: c'est à dire, la création d'ouvrages de référence à l'esthétique unique, dont l'objectif reste: *clarté* et *simplicité*.

En effet, nous sommes convaincus qu'un ouvrage peut être informatif tout en restant scientifiquement exact sans sacrifier la clarté du langage. En fait, un livre doit être facile à comprendre pour s'imposer en tant que référence. La quantité d'informations qu'il détient n'est pas le plus important, tant que le livre reste clair et précis. A cette fin, chaque chapitre du livre "Aquarium plants" a une barre informative présentant les spécificités de chaque variété dans un format qui permet une consultation d'un seul coup d'oeil. Nos fidèles lecteurs reconnaîtront cette barre que l'on retrouve par exemple dans l'ouvrage "Marine Aquarium Companion." Ce résumé, mélange d'icone et de texte, est tellement apprécié par nos lecteurs que nous en feront un outil inconditionnel de tous nos ouvrages de référence.

Nous ne soulignerons jamais assez le fait qu'un texte long n'est pas un but en soi-même. En fait, la concision est plutôt une qualité réelle. Ainsi, les lecteurs seront heureux de recevoir un maximum d'informations en un minimum de texte. Toutefois, il reste des lecteurs qui jugent un ouvrage à la quantité de texte plutôt qu'à la qualité des informations données. Nos ouvrages contiennent des informations pratiques, concises dans le format le plus simple possible.

Plusieurs données dans ce livre ont été résumées avec soin dans le souci de la concision. Brad Maclean qui fait partie de l'établissement Florida Aquatic Nursery (le plus grand producteur de plantes d'aquarium des Etats Unis) les a toutes vérifiées. Le docteur Leo Morin des laboratoires Seachem, Inc., a examiné de nombreuses informations concernant la chimie de l'eau.

Pour finir, nous souhaitons que ce livre apportera une aide précieuse à toute personne souhaitant monter un aquarium avec des plantes aquatiques, que ce soit également dans sa maintenance, son entretien ou la sélection des plantes d'aquarium. Mais surtout, nous espérons que ce livre vous procurera de nombreuses heures de plaisir.

# Voorwoord

"Aquarium Plants: The Practical Guide" is het vierde boek van "New Life Publications" en het eerste dat de wereld der aquariumplanten onderzocht. Het onderwerp sluit nauw aan bij onze andere boeken nl. de "Cichlids: The Pictorial Guide" boeken.

Planten zijn een vitale componente in een gezond aquarium ecosysteem. Vissen profiteren van planten en omgekeerd: het is een voorbeeld van een grote interactieve natuurrelatie.

Het spreekt voor zich dat wij in een aquarium niet hetzelfde sluitend ecosysteem kunnen opzetten als in de natuur. Hoewel, er bestaan middelen om te komen tot een goed gedijend aquarium. Mijn bedoeling bij het schrijven van dit boek is derhalve: hobbyisten voorzien van informatie over practische en bewezen methoden om een mooi aangeplant aquarium te verkrijgen. Gewapend met aangepaste kennis kan iedereen op een betrouwbare manier beschikken over mooie aquariumplanten.

In het gedeelte "methoden vergelijken" zal je foto's zien van een plant die ik buiten in het zonlicht kweekte (in stromend water en met een groep zwaarddragers zonder gebruik te maken van de kweektechnieken die in dit boek worden vermeld. Ik plaatste dezelfde plant in een aquarium dat werd ingericht volgens de principes van dit boek. U kan zelf de resultaten beoordelen.

In 1997 bleken hobbyisten in Europa en Azië goed de kunst te beheersen om een prachtig aangeplant aquarium te onderhouden. US-hobbyisten, minder bedreven in het houden van aquarium planten, maken elk jaar toch vorderingen. Ik ben overtuigd dat binnen enkele jaren (misschien met de hulp van dit boek) die USA-hobbyisten evengoed in staat zullen zijn om, zoals dat in elk ander land het geval is, een degelijk beplant aquarium op te zetten.

Een goed voorbeeld van een domein waarin hobbyisten wereldwijd grote vooruitgang hebben geboekt is de kennis en de techniek bij het houden van zeewateraquaria. In de vroege zeventiger jaren gebruikten zeewateraquarianen gebleekte koraal en onefficiënte kiezel filters in hun aquaria. Maar dank zij de moderne technieken van droog/nat filters, eiwitafschuimers en UV licht is het houden van een zeewateraquarium op vandaag uitvoerbaarder geworden. Het is nodig om een gelijkaardige vooruitgang te boeken in het houden van aquariumplanten: momenteel moet de overgang van oude methoden naar meer moderne, gemakkelijker zijn voor een beplant aquarium dan het was met een zeewateraquarium.

Zoals alle boeken, uitgegeven door "New Life Publication," is "Aquarium Plants: The Practical Guide" ook ontworpen als een betrouwbaar naslagwerk voor de vele variëteiten in het brede domein van de aquariumplanten. Alle planten opgenomen in dit boek worden geillustreerd met prachtige - belangrijker nog-natuurgetrouwe foto's die het handelsmerk zijn van onze boeken.

Het vullen van een boek met foto's van echte planten in top-conditie resulteert in een betrouwbaar naslagwerk dat meteen ook dient om de tekorten van kunststofplanten te verduidelijken. Ik denk dat hobbyisten geneigd zijn om namaakplanten te gebruiken, enkel om die éne reden: ze hebben geen voldoende kennis hoe ze planten gezond kunnen houden en daarom lijkt het gebruik van namaakplanten de eenvoudigste oplossing. Dat is een houding waarin dit boek hopelijk verandering kan brengen. Door enkele eenvoudige richtlijnen voor onderhoud en door het tonen van beelden van echte planten in al hun pracht, hoop ik hobbyisten te overtuigen dat er geen enkele reden bestaat om namaak te verkiezen boven echt. Laat het ons duidelijk

stellen : hoe goed namaak ook is, het blijft namaak! Meer nog, namaakplanten zorgen niet voor fotosynthese (zuurstof voorziening) noch helpen ze bij het neutraliseren van stikstofhoudend afval. Echte planten vervullen deze functies wel wat o.a. het ontstaan van problemen bij het inrichten van een nieuw aquarium vermindert. In een nieuw aquarium immers kan nitriet ($NO_2$) zeer snel toenemen en is het risico op vissterfte zeer groot. Plaatst men planten vooraleer de vis uit te zetten dan wordt voor die vissen de omgeving al een heel stuk geconditioneerd. Vissen redden het beter in een aquarium met echte planten dan in een namaakomgeving.

Een andere toelichting door "Aquarium Plants: The Practical Guide" is het verkeerdelijk gebruik van moeras-, terrarium- en andere niet-waterplanten in aquariums.

Door inlichtingen te verschaffen over echte aquariumplanten hoop ik de consument te informeren nopens wat een plant zal doen gedijen in de onderwater omgeving van een aquarium. Bovendien bevat het boek een hoofdstuk over niet-aquarium planten dat moet dienen als een soort wat-te-mijden-lijst. Het bevat foto's als herkenning wat hobbyisten een goed zicht geeft op wat ze beter vermijden.

Zoals altijd is het doel van "New Life Publications" om aan hobbyisten zo klaar en duidelijk mogelijk de informatie te verstrekken die hen aanmoedigt bij het opzetten en onderhouden van hun aquarium. De filosofie die wij aanhielden bij het ontwerpen van "Aquarium Plants: The Practical Guide" is dezelfde die we volgden bij het publiceren van andere boeken: unieke en mooie boeken creëren die zowel kunstzinnig als een krachtig informatieinstrument zijn.

Een ander gezichtspunt in onze filosofie is duidelijkheid en eenvoud. Ik meen dat boeken wetenschappelijk accuraat en informatief kunnen zijn zonder op te offeren aan duidelijkheid. Ik ben ervan overtuigd dat, om krachtig-informatief over te komen, een boek makkelijk te begrijpen moet zijn. Het is niet de vraag hoeveel gegevens in een boek worden gestouwd, wèl of ze duidelijk en eenvoudig bruikbaar zijn. Alle onderwerpen in het "Aquarium Plants" hoofdstuk van dit boek hebben een informatiebar met belangrijke, overzichtelijk uitgewerkte gegevens hoe je elke variëteit kan houden. Kenners van onze andere boeken zullen zich deze informatiebar herinneren uit onze "Marine Aquarium Companion". Deze op beeld en tekst gebaseerde samenvatting voor elke variëteit had zoveel succes dat het logisch lijkt om het als imago voor al onze naslagwerken te behouden.

Een optie die we in al onze boeken aanhouden is, dat het geven van veel tekst geen doel op zichzelf mag zijn. Het tegendeel is waar. Lezers wensen een maximum aan informatie met zo weinig mogelijk tekst. Veel lezers hebben een "papiertermen" mentaliteit waarin hoeveelheid tekst belangrijker is dan de kwaliteit van de gegevens erin. Onze boeken bevatten gecondenseerde, practische informatie op de meest eenvoudige manier voorgesteld.

Meerdere informatiedata in dit boek werden zorgvuldig nagekeken op nauwkeurigheid. Brad Maclean van de "Florida Aquatic Nursery (de grootste plantenproducent van de VS) verifieerde de gegevens voor elke variëteit. Dr Leo Morin van de "Seachem Labs, Inc." verifieerde veel van de informatie in de boeken in verband met de scheikundige samenstelling van water.

We hopen dat dit boek voor u een waardevolle bron wordt bij het opzetten, onderhoud en de keuze van de aquariumplanten. Maar, even belangrijk, we hopen dat "Aquarium Plants: The Practical Guide" u veel uren plezier zal bezorgen.

# Introduction to Aquarium Plants

Welcome to the world of aquarium plants. Keeping a planted aquarium can be a rewarding hobby that — despite what you may have heard — is not particularly difficult. Keep in mind a few simple rules and facts and you'll be well on your way to a flourishing underwater garden that will provide beauty and hours of relaxation.

The information presented here is straightforward, and we have kept the technical jargon to a minimum. As you will see, basically anybody can have a "green thumb."

## Photosynthesis & Your Aquarium Plants.

When setting up your tank, remember how important photosynthesis is in maintaining healthy plants. Photosynthesis is the process by which plants use chlorophyll with the aid of light energy synthesize water, carbon (which can be found in carbon dioxide or other carbon compounds) and various other nutrients into simple sugars. These simple sugars provide energy for the plant's growth and maintenance.

A major by-product of photosynthesis is oxygen. Therefore, during periods of light, plants draw carbon dioxide ($CO_2$) out of the water and release oxygen into the water. Yet, like animals, plants also continuously *respire:* they draw oxygen from the water and release $CO_2$ into the environment. During periods of light (when photosynthesis takes place), the amount of oxygen released into the water dwarfs the amount of oxygen consumed by the plants. Likewise, the amount of $CO_2$ released is insignificant compared to the plants' oxygen output.

During dark periods, there *is no* photosynthesis. This means that as the plant respires, it consumes oxygen and releases carbon dioxide.

It is important for the hobbyist to be aware of these processes and take them into account when setting up a tank. The following few sections describe simple ways to accomplish this.

**Lighting — Natural vs. Artificial:** It is a good idea to place a planted aquarium away from natural sources of sunlight and instead rely on artificial lighting. This seems to go against common sense, but, keep in mind that plants need a fairly substantial amount of light per day and many plants require a certain intensity of light. These factors are hard to control with natural light, but are easy to control with artificial light.

**Light Intensity:** Different plants have different light requirements. Improper lighting (usually too little light) is the most common cause of death in aquarium plants. The following recommendations are for a tank that is up to a maximum of 50 cm (20") deep using a full-spectrum flourescent light.

*Plants that require subdued light:*
    *approx. 1.5–2.0 watts-per-3.78 liters (1 gallon)*

*Plants that require moderate light:*
    *approx. 2.5–3.0 watts-per-3.78 liters (1 gallon)*

*Plants that require bright light:*
    *approx. 3.5–4.5 watts-per-3.78 liters (1 gallon)*

Light intensity reduces substantially as the rays reach the bottom of an aquarium, so I recommend that you use metal halide or mercury vapor lamps for aquariums more than 50 cm (20") deep. They provide more intense light than flourescent tubes with similar wattages do. Keep in mind that these metal halide or mercury vapor

lamps are significantly hotter than flourescent tubes, so you need to suspend the fixtures about 30 cm (12") above an open-topped (no hood) aquarium. If you use a hood, keep the lights (even flourescent lights) as far away from the water as possible and provide ample ventilation in your hood. Unless you have a chiller unit, you should never mount metal halide lights inside a hood.

**Light Duration:** I recommend a light period of 10–12 hours. Of course, one convenient way of providing consistent lighting is an automatic timer. Setting the timer to provide light between approximately 11:00 A.M. and 11:00 P.M. provides the plants with enough light, and it allows you to enjoy your tank during the evening hours.

**Providing Carbon Dioxide:** As mentioned earlier, carbon is an essential part of photosynthesis and must be provided if aquarium plants are to remain healthy. Carbon Dioxide ($CO_2$) desolves quickly in water and is the simplest carbon compound for plants to utilize. I recommend using a $CO_2$ injection system to provide aquarium plants with sufficient carbon.

Many aquarists (particularly in the U.S.) believe that fish respiration (in a tank containing both plants and fish) is all that is needed to provide $CO_2$ for aquarium plants. But there is more to consider. If you intend to put an extremely large population of fish in a tank, their respiration may provide enough $CO_2$ for the plants in the tank, but the consequences of overstocking the tank outweigh any benefits. Fish are animals. Animals produce waste. A large population of fish would produce tremendous amounts of ammonia and nitrogenous by-products. Both compounds are usable by plants, but an excess of them can cause uncontrollable algae blooms and prove to be toxic to the fish. If you are still skeptical about the advantage of using a $CO_2$ injection system, simply look at an aquarium with one installed. You will notice small beads of oxygen rising from the plants, which indicates that a healthy level of photosynthesis is taking place. You will rarely see this in tanks without this system.

In addition to providing plants with a carbon source, a $CO_2$ injection system also allows hobbyists to easily and dependably maintain a desired pH level (generally 6.7-7.0 pH) in within their aquarium environment.

**Carbon Dioxide Amounts:** Generally speaking, a good level of $CO_2$ in an aquarium is around 8 parts-per-million (ppm). This can be checked with a carbon dioxide test kit or by simply observing the behavior of any fish you may have in the tank. If you see your fish "gasping" or breathing rapidly, or if they swim toward the surface for air, the level of $CO_2$ may be too high. Remember, while carbon dioxide is good for plants, excessive amounts can kill your fish! You should balance the needs of all the organisms in your tank. Luckily, $CO_2$ poisoning is not very likely in a planted aquarium.

If the $CO_2$ levels in your tank are indeed excessive, vigorous aeration of the water will quickly correct the problem. By aerating your tank with an air pump, you allow $CO_2$ to escape and be replaced by oxygen.

**Light and CO2:** You may recall that during periods of light, plants draw more $CO_2$ from the water than they release; during dark periods they *only* release $CO_2$ into the water. Therefore, your light and $CO_2$ injection system should work together. When the lights are

# Introduction to Aquarium Plants

on, the $CO_2$ injection system should also be operating. When you turn the aquarium lights off, it is *imperative that you also deactivate your carbon dioxide injection system.*

Light without sufficient $CO_2$ will reduce the level of photosynthesis taking place. Conversely, carbon dioxide without sufficient light will reduce photosynthesis and cause too much $CO_2$ to be dissolved into the water.

A balance must be maintained between light levels and the amount of $CO_2$ being injected into the system in order for sufficient levels of photosynthesis to take place.

**Nighttime Aeration:** Like $CO_2$, aeration must be controlled according to the light. During the photosynthesis period (when lights are on), the tank must not be aerated. Aeration (as mentioned earlier) causes the $CO_2$ in the water to escape, which is beneficial during the night period, when plants *only* respire (consume oxygen and release carbon dioxide). One simple way to make sure the aeration and light cycles are timed appropriately is to connect your air pump to a timer set on a schedule opposite to that of your lights.

## Temperature

Aquarium plants and most tropical fish thrive in a temperature range of approximately 23°–28° Celsius (74°–83° farenheight). Hobbyists who live in areas that experience extreme temperatures during the year should invest in equipment that will keep their aquarium water within this optimal range.

In areas where seasonal temperatures drop below about 20° Celsius (68° farenheight), it is necessary to keep your aquarium in a heated room or to install a heater in the tank. In areas where temperatures reach 32° Celsius (90° farenheight) or above, it is necessary to keep your planted aquarium in an air-conditioned room or — as an even better solution — install a chiller in the tank.

However, even in hot areas where it is necessary to cool the water (via air-conditioning or a chiller), a heater under the substrate of your tank is necessary to help create vertical circulation. The details of this will be discussed in the section *Circulation and Heating the Substrate.* Finally, as with higher levels of light, increased temperatures accelerate metabolic activities and photosynthesis, so it would be wise to increase the light, $CO_2$, and nutrients in proportion to the increase in the temperature.

## Nutrients and the Substrate

Because of decaying organic matter and — if your planted aquarium contains fish — animal waste, aquariums usually contain an abundant amount of nutrients such as ammonium, nitrate, and phosphate. These basic, abundant substances are the *major nutrients* needed by aquarium plants. Of these *major nutrients,* only potassium (K) is not naturally produced in your tank and will have to be added.

Another important group of nutrients are called *micronutrients.* These include iron (Fe), copper (Cu), magnesium (Mg), zinc (Zn), boron (Br), sodium (Na), sulfur (S), and manganese (Mn). Although potassium (K) is not truly a *micronutrient,* it is included in many micronutrient plant supplement products.

**Providing Micronutrients:** Iron is one of the most vital micronutrients because it is a component of the enzyme that supports photosynthesis. Without adequate iron, the cell stops producing chlorophyll, and the leaves turn a sickly yellowish color. Of course, without sufficient chlorophyll, the level of photosynthesis needed for plants to thrive is not possible.

Iron supplements are available through dealers, as are supplements containing all the necessary micronutrients. Liquid supplements should be added once or twice a week. If you use supplements in tablet form, they should be placed in the gravel near the root system of the target plant. The manufacturer's instructions should tell you how frequently to add new tablets.

Adding liquid micronutrient supplements to the water every week allows plants — particularly exposed-root and rootless plants — to absorb adequate amounts of these substances both through their leaves and their stems.

**Substrate and Micronutrients:** In a planted aquarium, a substrate serves two functions: it provides deep-rooted plants with a continuous supply of micro-nutrients, and it prevents micronutrients from being oxidized. Therefore, it is important to create an *anaerobic* (oxygen poor) zone in your planted aquarium. This is of most benefit to deep-rooted plants.

**Circulation and Heating the Substrate:** The substrate can also heat the water and promote circulation in the tank. In the following section (*How to Build the Substrate*), I recommend placing a heating cable on the bottom layer of the substrate. The heat from the cable creates a very slow *vertical* ( from the bottom of the tank to the top) current of water.

This current is generated due to the fact that heated water rises, and colder water sinks. The circulation in the tank is maintained by this pattern of heated molecules rising and cooler molecules sinking.

I can't stress enough the fact that even if you live in a hot area and you actively cool your aquarium's water, you still need a heater under the substrate because the tank needs vertical circulation. If you cool the water in your tank by keeping it in an air-conditioned room, set the heating cable's thermostat to a minimum of 2° Celsius (4° F.) above the room temperature. This will cause the heating cable to activate. Also, the room should be cooler than the temperature you wish to maintain in your tank.

If you use a chiller, however, the room temperature does not need to be adjusted. Simply set the heating cable's thermostat to several degrees above that of the chiller, and set the chiller's thermostat to a few degrees below your tank's target temperature.

Gentle circulation of the tanks water helps prevent the buildup of nitrogenous waste by the process I will now describe: first, the circulation causes water to constantly flow through the upper area of the substrate, which is composed of more permeable gravel. This upper layer is an "aerobic zone"—which means it is oxygen-rich. This area contains *aerobic* bacteria. The ammonia in the water that flows through the upper, permeable substrate is oxidized into *nitrite* ($NO_2$) by the bacteria. This nitrite is then converted by other bacteria into *nitrate* ($NO_3$). Appropriately, these two groups of bacteria are called *nitrifying* bacteria.

Some of the $NO_3$ filters down into the "anaerobic (oxygen poor) zone" discussed earlier. This area must have little current. The anaerobic *denitrifying bacteria* in this area convert the $NO_3$ into nitrogen gas. The bacteria do this by using the oxygen in the $NO_3$. The metabolism of these bacteria—like all organisms—require oxygen. The resulting nitrogen gas then dissipates into the atmosphere.

# Introduction to Aquarium Plants

**How to Build the Substrate:** The following is a guide to building a substrate with heating, aerobic, and anaerobic zones.

*(1) The Bottom:* First, lay a heating cable on the bottom of the tank in a zig-zag pattern.

*(2) The Anaerobic Zone:* Next, put an approximately 1.5 cm (½") layer of *fine* river gravel (ideally the gravel should be coarser than silica sand) on top of the heating cable. On top of this layer, sprinkle *substrate additive* (follow the manufacturer's instructions). Add another 1.5 cm (½") layer of *fine* river gravel. The two layers form the anaerobic zone, where the water flows more slowly than it does in the aerobic zone.

*(3) The Aerobic Zone:* Finally, add about 8 cm (3") of washed, porous (or larger grain) gravel to the substrate. This top layer is the aerobic zone, through which the waters flow more freely than in the anaerobic zone. Keep in mind that there must be a current (provided by the heater) or all the anaerobic bacteria in the lower substrate will not thrive, creating a "dead zone." In addition, this "dead zone" will trap various chemicals that will rot the roots, turning them black.

## Setting Up Your Tank

After you set up the substrate, you should fill the tank from ⅓ to ½ full. This allows for easy planting. When introducing the water, you don't want to disturb the substrate by shooting a strong stream of water directly into the bottom of the tank.

One way to avoid this is to use a plate or your hand to block the stream so that the water flows evenly and gently into the aquarium.

Once the water fills a portion of the tank, you can plant your plants. Plant each species in one concentrated area rather than scattering them all around the aquarium. This will reflect the way the plants grow naturally. After planting, you can finish filling the tank.

## Water Quality & Chemistry

**Filtration:** Filtration serves a few important roles in your aquarium. First, filtration helps maintain the clarity of the water in your tank. Not only is clear water more attractive than clouded water, but it also allows light to penetrate to the bottom of the aquarium.

Second, the current created by filtration helps prevent (and washes away) debris from settling on the leaves of the plant. Debris is often harmful because it can block plant pores (stomata) and thus hinder plant respiration. In extreme cases, a coating of debris can interfere with the process of photosynthesis.

Third, many aquarists believe that the constant movement of plants in the current created by filtration helps to strengthen the structure of the plants. Be sure that filtration in your aquarium is accomplished *without aeration*. (I discussed in previous sections the need to control aeration.) The output tube of the filtration device should be submerged well below the water's surface to prevent it from causing surface agitation, which would allow $CO_2$ to escape into the atmosphere. Most dealers carry some form of submersible powerhead filter, as well as external cannister filters (with tubes that go under the water). Your choice really depends upon your set up. Cannister filters are good for densely populated tanks.

**Water Chemistry (What is pH, dKH, & dH?):** Most hobbyists understand that pH is the concentration of hydrogen ions (H+) in the water. In fact, pH stands for *power of hydrogen* in latin.

If there is a high concentration of hydrogen ions in the water, the water is considered to be *acidic* (below pH 7.0). If there are low concentrations of hydrogen ions in the water, it is *alkaline* (above pH 7.0). Decaying organic matter (as well as organic waste) can make water more acidic.

Neutral pH is measured as pH 7.0. For a majority of aquarium plants, an ideal pH is from pH 6.7 – pH 7.0 because most of the plants come from areas with acidic water.

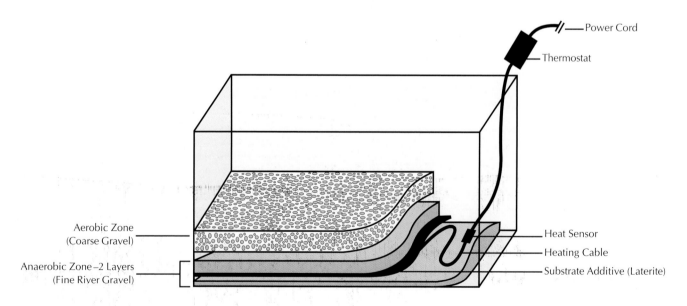

Aerobic Zone
(Coarse Gravel)

Anaerobic Zone – 2 Layers
(Fine River Gravel)

Power Cord

Thermostat

Heat Sensor

Heating Cable

Substrate Additive (Laterite)

## Diagram: The Substrate

# Introduction to Aquarium Plants

An additional benefit of keeping a slightly acidic planted aquarium is that in water with pH lower than 7.0, there is a higher concentration of hydrogen. This causes more ionic ammonium ($NH_4+$), which is relatively safe, to be formed. However, in higher pH water, more non-ionic ammonia ($NH_3$), which is very toxic, is formed.

Less understood are dKH and dH. Even many advanced hobbyists are not completely sure of the differences between dKH or dH. Part of the problem is that the literature describing these two often uses complex terminology such as *general hardness, temporary hardness, permanent hardness, GH,* and *KH.* I will try to avoid that here.

First, dKH is the measure of *carbonate hardness,* which is the concentration of *carbonates* and *bicarbonates* in the water. An ideal dKH value is approximately 3 degrees (3°). The dKH can be measured with commercially available test kits. Make sure that any test kit you buy measures carbonate and bicarbonate hardness (dKH)— *not* calcium and magnesium hardness (dH).

If the dKH is too low, you can add tap water (which has carbonate hardness). Use *sodium bicarbonate (baking soda )* if you still need to increase the dKH, but this is generally not necessary unless you are using distilled or purified water in the tank.

Usually, dKH values are too high rather than too low. If the dKH is high, add distilled water or water that has been purified by the *deionized and R.O. method.* These two purifying methods are described in the next section. Be aware that not all the methods of creating soft water reduce the dKH.

Traditionally, dH refer to *water hardness,* Which is the concentration of calcium ions (Ca+) and magnesium ions (Mg+) in the water. If the concentration of Ca+ and Mg+ ions in the water is high(indicated by a high dH reading), the water is considered hard. Low concentrations of these two ions (a low dH value) means the water is considered soft.

## Water Chemistry—Creating Soft Water:
In most cases, the water available to hobbyists for use in their aquariums is hard, so creating hard water is not usually much of an issue. However, if you do need to create hard water, commercially available chemicals can quickly and easily "harden" the water. For most aquarists, the main problem is creating *soft water,* which has low dKH and dH.

*Rainwater.* Because rain is usually devoid of Ca+, Mg+, and bicarbornates, it is often an ideal source of soft water. However, in industrialized areas, there are high concentrations of pollutants such as sulfur dioxide and hydrogen chloride that inevitably get into the rainwater.

If you live in a fairly unpolluted area, rainwater may be a good bet. However, you will still want to add some *non-chlorinated* tap water to obtain the proper dKH and dH.

*Distilled Water.* This form of water is the most widely available form of pure water. A little *too* pure, in fact; because it contains basically no minerals and only a few dissolved gases, distilled water disrupts the osmotic balance between the water and living organisms.

The balance is disrupted because minerals and other substances will leech out of the organism and into the water. The concentrations of these minerals and substances tend to become distributed equally on the outside and inside of the organism's semipermeable membrane. This equalization can kill the organism (including plants). So if you're going to use distilled water, mix it with tap water to obtain the desired dKH. For a large aquarium, however, distilled water is very expensive and is not a cost-effective solution.

*Reverse Osmosis (R.O.) Method.* The reverse osmosis unit creates soft water, which is similar to distilled water, by using pressure to force ions through a semi-permeable membrane against the osmotic gradient.

Keep in mind that the water purified with a reverse osmosis unit will never be as pure as distilled water. Also, the units available to hobbyists generally can't provide enough pressure to create truly pure water. However, they can remove enough calcium ions (Ca+), magnesium ions (Mg+), and bicarbonates for the water to be used in planted aquariums.

*Peat Moss.* Peat moss softens water by binding with Ca+ and Mg+ while releasing *tannic acid* and *gallic acid.* This increases the acidity of the water, which causes some bicarbonates to be converted to $CO_2$, which lowers the dKH. Athough it is one of the most cost-effective methods for softening the water, peat moss does have some disadvantages. It is slower than most other methods and often not as thorough; it may not sufficiently lower the dKH. Also, it turns the water a yellowish color.

This yellow cast to the water can be removed by using high-grade carbon in a mechanical filter. However, carbon does increase both dKH and pH by releasing carbonates into the water. How much it releases into the water depends on the ash content of the carbon.

## Resin Softening Methods:
Resin is used to soften water in two methods — the *Sodium Softening Method* and the *Deionization Method.* Of the two, the *Deionization Method* is by far superior. The *Sodium Softening Method* is essentially useless in softening water for plants. It simply replaces a set of cations (Ca+ and Mg+) with another cation (Na+). However, people often mistakenly think that if water does not contain calcium and magnesium ions, it is suitable for planted aquariums.

*Sodium Softening Method.* In this method, a substance called *cationic resin in sodium form* is used commercially to soften hard water. Yet, chemically speaking, this substance does not remove all the cations (such as sodium) that also contribute to the hardness, and it lacks the ability to remove *carbonates* or *bicarbonates.* In other words, it doesn't lower the dKH.

The reason this method is used commercially is that water softened in this manner causes soap to produce more suds than it does in hard water, thus reducing water, soap, and other costs.

*Deionization Method.* This method of softening aquarium water is better than the Sodium Softening Method. Two resins are used in deionization: a *cationic resin in hydrogen form* (consisting of positively charged ions) and *anionic resin in hydroxyl form* (negative ions).

The cationic resin replaces positively charged ions in the water (such as Ca+ and Mg+) with hydrogen ions (H+). Likewise, the anionic resin replaces the *chloride, bicarbonates,* and *carbonates* with the negatively charged molecule OH-. A side effect of this process is that the resulting free H+ and OH- combine to become water ($H_2O$).

Water purified in this manner eliminates both *Ca+ and Mg+ hardness* (dH) and *carbonate hardness* (dKH). In fact, the resulting water is similar to distilled water. As with distilled water, it is imperative that you add tap water to obtain the proper dKH.

Also, once the resins are saturated with chlorides and carbonates, they need to be either recharged with strong acid or replaced with new resin. I strongly recommend that you do not try to recharge the resin. Acid is extremely dangerous.

# Introduction to Aquarium Plants

**pH, dKH, dH and $CO_2$:** The carbonate hardness (dKH), acidity and amount of carbon dioxide in the water all work together to determine the overall quality of the water. Each affects the other. The pH of your aquarium water is determined by the levels of both $CO_2$ and dKH. The $CO_2$ generates carbonic acid, which lowers the pH; the dKH (carbonate hardness) acts as a buffer that stabilizes the pH. If the dKH is at the ideal level of about 3° (see earlier sections), it prevents the pH from dropping below about pH 6.7 when $CO_2$ is introduced. If the dKH is too low, a small amount of $CO_2$ will drop the pH far below 6.7 to a dangerous level. If the dKH is too high, even large amounts of $CO_2$ will not reduce the alkalinity (high pH).

The dKH level can be indirectly determined by testing the pH. If $CO_2$ is injected, the pH should drop readily. If the pH drops readily but doesn't go below 6.7, the dKH is ideal. If the pH drops below 6.7, the dKH is too low. Conversely, if injecting $CO_2$ does not readily drop the pH to 6.7, then the dKH is too high.

Finally, if you maintain the proper dKH value ( approximately 3°), the dH will automatically fall within an acceptable range for "soft water." This is why I have not spent much time discussing dH. All the methods of softening water (via controlling the dKH) just described will also lower the dH. All these methods reduce both the concentration of bicarbonates in the water (dKH) and the concentration of Ca+ and Mg+ (dH). The one exception is the *Sodium Softening Method*; it is not recommended.

**Environmental Factors & Water Quality:** Many decorations you may decide to put in your tank (driftwood, rocks, and gravel) can change the quality and chemistry of your aquarium water. For example, some rocks and gravel may bleed calcium into the water, and driftwood contains various chemicals that are released into the tank. I suggest boiling or extended soaking for driftwood and choose rocks and gravel that do not contain calcium or minerals that will increase the carbonate hardness (dKH) of the water.

## Algae & Snail Control

**Algae Control:** Anyone who has kept an aquarium is familiar with the frustration of algae growth. Not only is it unattractive, but it can hinder plant respiration and photosynthesis by covering the plants' leaves. Especially beware the smooth, dark-green gelatinous film called blue-green algae. Under conditions of high nitrate and phosphate levels, blue-green algae grow at an extremely rapid rate and can quickly smother plants. Of all the algae, this type appears to be the most difficult to eradicate since there do not seem to be any fish that will eat it readily. However, one product to my knowledge that will eliminate blue-green algae as well as other algae — *Health Guard,* is made by Seachem Labs and is safe to use with both fish and plants. Of course, the best approach is a preventative one: don't allow nitrate and phosphate levels to reach such high levels in your tank. Rampant algae growth seems to be a particular problem in newly setup aquariums. Here are a few suggestions to help control algae in your tank:

(1) Introduce algae-eating fish such as *Otocinclus, Epalzeorhynchus siamensis,* dwarf plecostomus, whiptail cats, other sucker-mouth fish (Loricariidae family), and most livebearers (Poeciliidae family). However, the types of plecostomus that grow very large are poor choices since many of them also eat plants. Corydoras catfish should also be introduced to stir up the gravel and prevent the algae from settling on the bottom of the tank.

You will want to introduce algae-eating fish as soon as your newly established planted aquarium is settled. Don't allow an algae problem to develop before adding the algae-eating fish. Most fish won't be able to eat enough in an already overgrown tank to be of much help. Feed the fish sparingly, so that they will feel compelled to eat the algae.

(2) Plant your aquarium densely from the beginning. Make sure to include many fast-growing plants. Many of the so-called "bunch plants" (plants that are grown from cuttings and sold in bunches) fall into this category. Rapidly growing plants inhibit algae growth.

(3) Change half of the water in the aquarium every week (or *at least* every other week) to eliminate the nitrogenous waste and phosphates that help algae thrive.

(4) If all else fails, some aquarists suggest treating the aquarium water with a very weak copper solution to bring the concentration of copper in the tank up to a level of 0.3–0.5 ppm. I can't stress enough that this is a last resort option.

Copper solutions that can kill algae can kill both aquarium plants and fish too. In fact, this method is extremely controversial. I don't recommend this method, but many commercial plant growers use copper solutions.

If you *do* decide to use this method, be aware of a few facts: a small percentage of plants can be killed by even this small dose of copper. These "copper sensitive" plants are indicated as such in the Information Bar for each species. More information on this can be found in the User's Guide section of this book.

Measure precisely when using copper; the life of your plants and fish depend on it. Also, when you are done, make sure to either change the water or use an activated carbon filter to remove the copper.

**Snail Control:** Most snails can be destructive in the planted aquarium. Snails such as Applesnails (*Ampullaria paludosa*) and Colombian Ramhorn Snails (*Marisa rotula*), have especially voracious appetites for plants. The mystery snails (*Ampullaria cuprina*), which are traditionally used in algae control, eat plants as well.

The basic method to help keep snails at bay is to simply add snail-eating fish to your aquarium. One such type includes the freshwater puffers. The downside of introducing these fish is that they are aggressive. They nip the other fish in your aquarium and will often eat small fish if they can catch them.

Clown loaches(*Botia macracantha*) and dwarf botias are better choices. A two-inch (6 cm) clown loach can easily eliminate small snails in the matter of days.

# Einführung zu Aquariumpflanzen

Willkommen in der Welt der Aquariumpflanzen. Die Haltung eines bepflanzten Aquariums kann ein lohnenswertes Hobby sein, das — im Gegensatz dazu, was Sie vielleicht gehört haben — gar nicht so schwer ist. Wenn Sie ein paar einfache Regeln und Tatsachen berücksichtigen, haben Sie schon bald einen blühenden Unterwassergarten, an dem Sie sich erfreuen und viele entspannende Stunden verbringen werden.

Die hier enthaltenen Informationen sind unkompliziert, und wir haben den technischen Jargon auf ein Minimum beschränkt. Wie Sie sehen werden, kann praktisch jedermann ein „Händchen für Pflanzen" haben.

## Photosynthese und Ihre Aquariumpflanzen

Vergessen Sie bei der Einrichtung Ihres Aquariums nicht, wie wichtig die Photosynthese ist, damit es Ihren Pflanzen gut geht. Die Photosynthese ist der Vorgang, in dem Pflanzen Chlorophyll mit Hilfe von Lichtenergie dazu verwenden, Wasser, Kohlenstoff (der in Kohlenstoffdioxid und anderen Kohlenstoffzusammensetzungen enthalten ist) und eine Reihe anderer Nährstoffe in einfache Zucker zu synthetisieren. Diese einfachen Zucker liefern die Energie für das Wachstum und die Pflege der Pflanzen.

Sauerstoff ist ein großes Nebenprodukt der Photosynthese. Aus diesem Grund entnehmen Pflanzen dem Wasser Kohlenstoff ($CO_2$), so lange Licht vorhanden ist, und geben Sauerstoff in das Wasser frei. Aber genau wie Tiere *respirieren* Pflanzen ebenfalls fortlaufend: sie entnehmen dem Wasser Sauerstoff und geben $CO_2$ in die Umgebung ab. So lange Licht vorhanden ist (wenn die Photosynthese stattfindet), stellt die Menge an Sauerstoff, die in das Wasser freigegeben wird, die Menge an Sauerstoff, die von den Pflanzen verbraucht wird, bei weitem in den Schatten. Genauso ist die Menge an $CO_2$, die freigegeben wird, im Vergleich zur Sauerstoffabgabe der Pflanzen unwesentlich.

Wenn es dunkel ist, findet *keine* Photosynthese statt. Dies bedeutet, daß die Pflanze, während sie respiriert, Sauerstoff verbraucht und Kohlendioxid freigibt.

Es ist wichtig, daß sich ein Hobby-Aquarianer dieser Prozesse bewußt ist und sie bei der Einrichtung seines Aquariums berücksichtigt. In den nächsten Abschnitten werden einfache Methoden beschrieben, mit denen dies erreicht wird.

**Beleuchtung — natürlich gegenüber künstlich:** Es ist eine gute Idee, ein bepflanztes Aquarium dort aufzustellen, wo es von natürlichem Sonnenlicht geschützt ist und sich anstatt dessen auf eine künstliche Beleuchtung zu verlassen. Dies scheint zwar gegen die Vernunft zu gehen, aber man darf nicht vergessen, daß Pflanzen jeden Tag eine relativ große Menge an Licht benötigen, und viele Pflanzen außerdem eine bestimmte Lichtintensität brauchen. Diese Faktoren sind mit natürlichem Licht schwer zu kontrollieren, aber mit einer künstlichen Beleuchtung kein Problem.

**Lichtintensität:** Unterschiedliche Pflanzen haben unterschiedliche Lichtanforderungen. Eine falsche Beleuchtung (meistens zu wenig Licht) ist der häufigste Grund für das Absterben von Aquariumpflanzen. Die nachstehenden Empfehlungen beziehen sich auf ein Aquarium, das *bis zu* 50 cm tief ist und eine Vollspektrum-Leuchtstofflampe zur Beleuchtung verwendet.

*Pflanzen, die gedämpftes Licht benötigen: circa 1,5–2,0 Watt pro 3,78 Liter*

*Pflanzen, die gemäßigtes Licht benötigen: circa 2,5–3,0 Watt pro 3,78 Liter*

*Pflanzen, die helles Licht benötigen: circa 3,5– 4,5 Watt pro 3,78 Liter*

Die Lichtintensität nimmt auf dem Weg der Lichtstrahlen zum Boden des Aquariums beträchtlich ab, daher empfehle ich Ihnen, in Aquarien, die tiefer als 50 cm sind, Halogen- oder Quecksilberdampflampen zu verwenden. Sie liefern ein intensiveres Licht als Leuchtstoffröhren mit ähnlichen Wattzahlen.

Vergessen Sie nicht, daß diese Halogen- oder Quecksilberdampflampen wesentlich heißer als Leuchtstoffröhren sind, und Sie die Lampen daher circa 30 cm über einem offenen Aquarium (ohne Haube) aufhängen müssen. Wenn Sie eine Haube benutzen, bringen Sie die Lampen (selbst Leuchtstofflampen) so weit wie möglich vom Wasser entfernt an, und sorgen Sie für eine ausreichende Ventilation in der Haube. Sie sollten niemals Halogenlampen in einer Haube unterbringen, es sei denn, sie verfügen über eine Kühleinheit.

**Beleuchtungsdauer:** Ich empfehle einen Beleuchtungszeitraum von 10 bis 12 Stunden. Ein automatischer Zeitschalter ist eine bequeme Methode, für eine beständige Beleuchtung zu sorgen. Wenn der Zeitschalter so eingestellt ist, daß er von circa 11.00 Uhr bis 23.00 Uhr für Licht sorgt, erhalten die Pflanzen genügend Licht, und Sie können sich auch in den Abendstunden an Ihrem Ihr Aquarium erfreuen.

**Versorgung mit Kohlendioxid:** Kohlenstoff ist, wie bereits erwähnt, ein wichtiger Bestandteil der Photosynthese und muß vorhanden sein, damit die Aquariumpflanzen gesund bleiben. Kohlen-dioxid ($CO_2$) löst sich schnell im Wasser auf und ist das einfachste Kohlenstoffgemisch, das Pflanzen nutzen können. Ich empfehle, ein $CO_2$-Injektionssystem zu verwenden, um Aquariumpflanzen mit ausreichendem Kohlenstoff zu versorgen.

Viele Aquarianer (besonders in den USA) glauben, daß die Fischrespiration (in einem Aquarium, das sowohl Pflanzen als auch Fische enthält) alleine dazu ausreicht, die Aquariumpflanzen mit $CO_2$ zu versorgen. Es müssen aber auch andere Aspekte in Betracht gezogen werden. Falls Sie vorhaben, Ihr Aquarium mit extrem vielen Fischen zu besiedeln, versorgt deren Respiration die Pflanzen im Aquarium eventuell mit genügend $CO_2$, aber die Konsequenzen eines Überbestands im Aquarium annullieren diese Vorteile. Fische sind Tiere. Tiere produzieren Ausscheidungen. Ein großer Fischbestand würde enorme Mengen Ammoniak und stickstoffhaltige Nebenprodukte erzeugen. Die Pflanzen können beide Gemische verwenden, aber ein Übermaß kann einen unkontrollierbare Algenbefall verursachen und sich für die Fische als giftig erweisen.

Falls Sie die Vorteile der Verwendung eines $CO_2$-Injektionssystems immer noch skeptisch betrachten, sehen Sie sich einfach einmal ein Aquarium an, in dem ein solches System installiert wurde. Sie werden kleine Sauerstoffperlen sehen, die von den Pflanzen aufsteigen, und dies weist darauf hin, daß ein gesundes Ausmaß an Photosynthese stattfindet. In Aquarien ohne dieses System ist dies selten zu beobachten.

Ein $CO_2$-Injektionssystem liefert Pflanzen nicht nur eine Kohlenstoffquelle, sondern ermöglicht es einem Hobby-Aquarianer außerdem, einfach und zuverlässig den gewünschten pH-Wert (generell 6,7–7,0 pH) in seinem Aquarium aufrecht zu erhalten.

**Kohlendioxidmengen:** Generell liegt ein gutes Niveau von CO2 in einem Aquarium bei rund 8 Teilen auf eine Million (ppm). Dies kann mit einem Kohlenstoff-Testkit oder durch Beobachten des Verhaltens der Fische im Aquarium überprüft werden. Wenn Sie sehen, daß Ihre Fische „nach Luft schnappen", sehr schnell atmen oder an die Oberfläche schwimmen, um Luft zu holen, ist das CO2-Niveau eventuell zu hoch. Denken Sie daran, daß Kohlendioxid zwar gut für Pflanzen ist, aber Ihre

# Einführung zu Aquariumpflanzen

Fische von zu großen Mengen getötet werden können. Sie sollten die Bedürfnisse *aller* Organismen in Ihrem Aquarium ins Gleichgewicht bringen. Glücklicherweise ist eine $CO_2$-Vergiftung in einem bepflanzten Aquarium nicht sehr wahrscheinlich.

Falls die $CO_2$-Niveaus in Ihrem Aquarium tatsächlich zu hoch sind, kann das Problem durch eine kräftige Anreicherung mit Sauerstoff schnell behoben werden. Wenn Sie Ihr Aquarium durch Verwendung einer Luftpumpe mit Sauerstoff anreichern, ermöglichen Sie, daß das $CO_2$ entweicht und von Sauerstoff ersetzt wird.

**Licht und $CO_2$:** Sie erinnern sich vielleicht daran, daß Pflanzen dem Wasser, während Licht herrscht, mehr $CO_2$ entnehmen als sie freigeben, und während der Dunkelheit scheiden Sie *nur* $CO_2$ in das Wasser aus. Aus diesem Grund sollten Ihr Beleuchtungs- und $CO_2$-Injektionssystem zusammenarbeiten. Wenn die Lampen eingeschaltet sind, sollte das $CO_2$-Injektionssystem ebenfalls arbeiten. Wenn Sie die Aquariumlampen ausschalten, ist es *unbedingt notwendig, das Kohlendioxid-Injektionssystem ebenfalls zu deaktivieren.*

Licht ohne genügend $CO_2$ reduziert das Ausmaß an Photosynthese, die stattfindet. Umgekehrt wird Kohlendioxid die Photosynthese ohne genügend Licht verringern und verursachen, daß sich zu viel $CO_2$ im Wasser auflöst.

Zwischen den Lichtniveaus und der Menge an CO2, die in das System injiziert wird, muß ein Gleichgewicht aufrecht erhalten werden, damit die Photosynthese im ausreichenden Ausmaß stattfinden kann.

**Nächtliche Anreicherung mit Sauerstoff:** Genau wie $CO_2$ muß auch die Anreicherung mit Sauerstoff je nach den Lichtbedingungen geregelt werden. Während der Photosyntheseperiode (wenn die Lampen eingeschaltet sind) darf das Aquarium nicht mit Sauerstoff angereichert werden. Die Anreicherung mit Sauerstoff verursacht (wie bereits erwähnt), daß das CO2 im Wasser entweicht, was nachts von Vorteil ist, wenn die Pflanzen *nur* respirieren (Sauerstoff verbrauchen und Kohlendioxid freigeben). Sie können problemlos sicherzustellen, daß die Zyklen für die Anreicherung mit Sauerstoff und die Beleuchtung zur richtigen Zeit stattfinden, wenn Sie die Luftpumpe an einen Zeitschalter anschließen, der so eingestellt wird, daß er sich umgekehrt zum Zeitschalter für die Lampen einschaltet.

## Temperatur

Aquariumpflanzen und die meisten tropischen Fische gedeihen in Temperaturen von circa 23 bis 28 Grad Celsius. Hobby-Aquarianer, die in Gegenden leben, in denen im Laufe des Jahres extreme Temperaturen auftreten, sollten in eine Ausrüstung investieren, mit der das Wasser in ihrem Aquarium innerhalb dieses optimalen Bereichs gehalten wird.

In Gegenden, in denen die Temperaturen unter 20 Grad Celsius abfallen, ist es notwendig, das Aquarium in einem beheizten Raum aufzustellen oder einen Heizer im Aquarium zu installieren. In Gegenden, wo die Temperaturen auf 32 Grad Celsius oder mehr klettern, muß das bepflanzte Aquarium in einen Raum mit Klimaanlage gestellt werden oder — eine sogar noch bessere Lösung — eine Kühlvorrichtung im Tank installiert werden.

Selbst in heißen Gegenden, , in denen das Wasser (durch eine Klimaanlage oder Kühlvorrichtung) abgekühlt werden muß, ist jedoch ein Heizer unter dem Substrat des Aquariums nötig, der dabei hilft, eine vertikale Zirkulation zu erzeugen. Die Details zu diesem Thema werden im Abschnitt *Zirkulation und Erwärmung des Substrats* angesprochen.

Letztlich beschleunigen höhere Temperaturen, genau wie höhere Lichtniveaus, die metabolischen Aktivitäten und die Photosynthese, daher ist es angeraten, das Licht, das $CO_2$ und die Nährstoffe proportional zur Temperatur zu erhöhen.

## Nährstoffe und das Substrat

Aquarien enthalten normalerweise aufgrund verfaulender organischer Stoffe und — falls sich Fische in Ihrem bepflanzten Aquarium befinden —aufgrund von Tierausscheidungen eine reichliche Menge an Nährstoffen, wie z.B. Ammonium, Nitrat und Phosphat. Diese grundlegenden, reichhaltigen Substanzen sind die *Hauptnährstoffe*, die Aquariumpflanzen benötigen. Von diesen *Hauptnährstoffen* wird nur Kalium (K) nicht natürlich im Aquarium produziert und muß zugegeben werden.

Eine andere wichtige Gruppe von Nährstoffen wird *Mikronährstoffe* genannt. Hierzu gehört Eisen (Fe), Kupfer (Cu), Magnesium (Mg), Zink (Zn), Boron (Br), Natrium (Na), Schwefel (S) und Mangan (Mn). Obwohl Kalium (K) nicht wirklich ein *Mikronährstoff* ist, ist es in vielen Produkten mit Mikronährstoffzusätzen für Pflanzen enthalten.

**Versorgung mit Mikronährstoffen:** Eisen ist einer der lebenswichtigsten Mikronährstoffe, weil es eine Komponente des Enzyms ist, das die Photosynthese unterstützt. Die Zellen hören ohne genügend Eisen mit der Produktion von Chlorophyll auf und die Blätter nehmen eine kränkliche gelbe Farbe an. Natürlich ist das Ausmaß an Photosynthese, das die Pflanzen zum Gedeihen benötigen, ohne genügend Chlorophyll nicht möglich.

Eisenzusätze sind bei Händlern erhältlich, genau wie Zusätze, die alle notwendigen Mikronährstoffe enthalten. Flüssige Zusätze sollten ein-bis zweimal pro Woche zugegeben werden. Falls Sie Zusätze in Tablettenform verwenden, sollten Sie im Kies in der Nähe der Wurzeln der fraglichen Pflanze gesteckt werden. In den Anleitungen des Herstellers sollte stehen, wie oft neue Tabletten zugegeben werden müssen.

Wenn Sie jede Woche flüssige Mikronährstoffzusätze in das Wasser geben, können Pflanzen — und besonders Pflanzen mit freiliegenden Wurzeln oder Pflanzen ohne Wurzeln — durch ihre Blätter und Stengel ausreichende Mengen dieser Substanzen absorbieren.

**Substrat und Mikronährstoffe:** Ein Substrat erfüllt in einem bepflanzten Aquarium zwei Funktionen: es versorgt tief verwurzelte Pflanzen fortlaufend mit Mikronährstoffen und verhindert, daß Mikronährstoffe oxidiert werden. Aus diesem Grund ist es wichtig, eine *anaerobe* (sauerstoffarme) Zone im bepflanzten Aquarium zu schaffen. Dies ist für tief verwurzelte Pflanzen äußerst vorteilhaft.

**Zirkulation und Erwärmung des Substrats:** Das Substrat kann außerdem das Wasser erwärmen und die Zirkulation im Aquarium fördern. Ich empfehle im nächsten Abschnitt (*Wie das Substrat aufgebaut wird*), ein Heizkabel auf die unterste Schicht des Substrats zu legen. Die Hitze des Kabels erzeugt eine sehr langsame, *vertikale* Wasserströmung (vom Boden des Aquariums nach oben). Diese Strömung entsteht, weil das erwärmte Wasser nach oben fließt und das kältere Wasser absinkt. Die Zirkulation im Aquarium wird aufrecht erhalten, weil sich diese erwärmten Moleküle nach oben bewegen und die kühleren Moleküle nach unten sinken.

Ich kann gar nicht genug betonen, daß Sie, selbst wenn Sie in einer heißen Gegend wohnen und das Wasser im Aquarium aktiv abkühlen, trotzdem einen Heizer unter dem Substrat benötigen, weil das Aquarium eine vertikale Zirkulation braucht. Wenn Sie das Wasser im Aquarium

# Einführung zu Aquariumpflanzen

dadurch kühlen, daß es in einem Raum mit Klimaanlage steht, stellen Sie den Thermostat des Heizkabels auf mindestens 2 Grad Celsius über der Zimmertemperatur ein. Hierdurch wird das Heizkabel aktiviert. Außerdem sollte die Temperatur im Raum kühler als die Temperatur sein, die Sie im Aquarium aufrecht erhalten wollen.

Wenn Sie eine Kühlvorrichtung verwenden, muß die Zimmertemperatur jedoch nicht angepaßt werden. Stellen Sie den Thermostat des Heizkabels einfach auf ein paar Grad mehr als die Temperatur der Kühlvorrichtung und den Thermostat der Kühlvorrichtung auf ein paar Grad weniger als die gewünschte Temperatur im Aquarium ein.

Die sanfte Zirkulation des Wassers im Aquarium trägt anhand des nachfolgend beschriebenen Vorgangs dazu bei, die Ansammlung stickstoffhaltiger Abfallstoffe zu verhindern. Erstens verursacht die Zirkulation, daß ständig Wasser durch den oberen Bereich des Substrats fließt, der aus durchlässigerem Kies besteht. Diese obere Schicht ist eine „aerobe Zone", das heißt, sie ist sauerstoffreich. Dieser Bereich enthält *aerobe* Bakterien. Das Ammoniak im Wasser, das durch das obere, durchlässige Substrat fließt, wird von den Bakterien in *Nitrit* ($NO_2$) oxidiert. Dieses Nitrit wird dann von anderen Bakterien in *Nitrat* ($NO_3$) umgewandelt. Dementsprechend werden diese zwei Gruppen von Bakterien *nitrifizierende* Bakterien genannt.

Ein Teil des Nitrats ($NO_3$) wird nach unten in die bereits erwähnte „anaerobe (sauerstoffarme) Zone" gefiltert. In diesem Bereich darf nur wenig Strömung herrschen. Die anaeroben, *entnitrifizierenden Bakterien* in diesem Bereich wandeln das $NO_3$ in Nitrogengas um. Die Bakterien nehmen dies unter Verwendung des Sauerstoffs im $NO_3$ vor. Der Metabolismus dieser Bakterien — wie aller Organismen — benötigt Sauerstoff. Das hieraus resultierende Nitrogengas löst sich dann in der Atmosphäre auf.

**Wie das Substrat aufgebaut wird:** Die nächsten Abschnitte enthalten Richtlinien für den Aufbau eines Substrats mit einer Beheizung und aeroben und anaeroben Zonen.

*(1) Der Boden:* Legen Sie zuerst ein Heizkabel in einem Zickzackmuster auf den Boden des Aquariums.

*(2) Die anaerobe Zone:* Verteilen Sie als nächstes eine circa 1,5 cm dicke Schicht aus *feinem* Flußkies (idealerweise sollte der Kies grober als Silikasand sein) auf dem Heizkabel. Streuen Sie *Substratzusatz* auf diese Schicht (Anleitungen des Herstellers befolgen). Geben Sie hierauf eine weitere 1,5 cm dicke Schicht aus *feinem* Flußkies. Die beiden Schichten formen die anaerobe Zone, in der das Wasser langsamer als in der aeroben Zone fließt.

*(3) Die aerobe Zone:* Geben Sie zum Schluß eine rund 8 cm dicke Schicht aus gewaschenem, porösen (oder körnigeren) Kies auf das Substrat. Diese oberste Schicht ist die aerobe Zone, durch die das Wasser ungehinderter als in der anaeroben Zone fließt. Denken Sie daran, daß eine Strömung (vom Heizer geliefert) vorhanden sein muß, andernfalls werden alle anaeroben Bakterien im unteren Substrat nicht gedeihen und eine „tote Zone" erzeugen. Darüber hinaus fängt diese „tote Zone" eine Reihe von Chemikalien ein, die verursachen, daß die Wurzeln verrotten und schwarz werden.

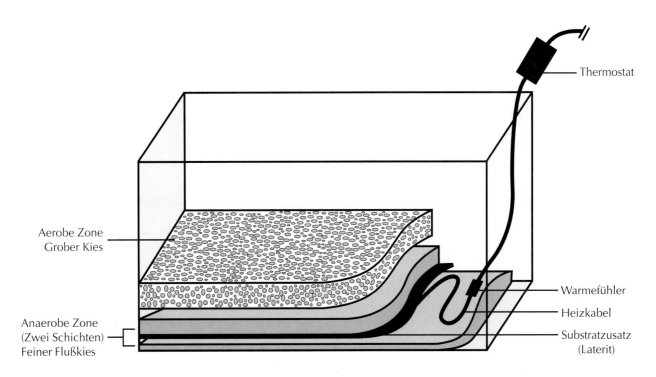

**Diagramm: Das Substrat**

# Einführung zu Aquariumpflanzen

## Einrichtung des Aquariums

Nachdem Sie das Substrat aufgebaut haben, sollten Sie das Aquarium zu einem Drittel bzw. zur Hälfte füllen. Hierdurch wird Ihnen das Anpflanzen einfach gemacht. Wenn Sie Wasser hinzugeben, dürfen Sie keinen starken Wasserstrahl direkt auf den Boden des Aquariums richten, weil sonst das Substrat aufgewühlt wird.

Sie können dieses Aufwühlen z.B. verhindern, wenn Sie den Wasserstrahl mit einem Teller oder Ihrer Hand so blockieren, daß das Wasser gleichmäßig und sanft in das Aquarium fließt.

Nachdem ein Teil des Aquariums mit Wasser gefüllt ist, können Sie Ihre Pflanzen anpflanzen. Pflanzen Sie jede Spezies in einem konzentrierten Bereich, anstatt alle Spezies im ganzen Aquarium zu verteilen. Dies spiegelt wieder, wie die Pflanzen in der Natur wachsen. Wenn Sie mit dem Anpflanzen fertig sind, können Sie den Rest des Aquariums füllen.

## Wasserqualität und Chemie

**Filterung:** Die Filterung spielt mehrere wichtige Rollen in Ihrem Aquarium. Erstens hilft die Filterung dabei, die Reinheit des Wassers aufrecht zu erhalten. Sauberes Wasser ist nicht nur attraktiver als trübes Wasser, sondern ermöglicht außerdem (was wichtig ist), daß das Licht bis zum Boden des Aquariums vordringen kann.

Zweitens wird durch Strömung, die durch die Filterung erzeugt wird, auch verhindert, daß sich Partikel auf den Blättern der Pflanzen ablagern (sie werden weggespült). Partikel sind oft schädlich, weil sie die Pflanzenporen (Stomata) verstopfen und hierdurch die Pflanzenrespiration behindern können. In extremen Fällen kann die Photosynthese durch eine Schicht aus Partikeln behindert werden. Drittens glauben viele Aquarianer, daß die ständige Bewegung der Pflanzen in der Strömung, die durch die Filterung erzeugt wird, dabei hilft, die Struktur der Pflanzen zu stärken.

Sie müssen darauf achten, daß die Filterung in Ihrem Aquarium *ohne Anreicherung mit Sauerstoff* erzielt wird. (Ich habe in vorgehenden Abschnitten die Notwendigkeit angesprochen, die Anreicherung mit Sauerstoff zu kontrollieren). Der Austrittsschlauch der Filterungsvorrichtung sollte sich weit unter der Wasseroberfläche befinden, um zu verhindern, daß die Oberfläche aufgewühlt wird, was erlauben würde, daß $CO_2$ in die Atmosphäre entweicht.

Die meisten Händler bieten sowohl motorisierte Unterwasserfilter als auch externe Kanisterfilter (mit Schläuchen, die im Wasser versenkt werden) an. Wofür Sie sich entscheiden, hängt von Ihrer Einrichtung ab. Kanisterfilter sind gut für dicht besiedelte Aquarien geeignet.

**Wasserchemie (Was bedeutet pH, dKH und dH?):** Die meisten Hobby-Aquarianer wissen, daß pH die Konzentration von Wasserstoffionen (H+) im Wasser ist. Tatsächlich bedeutet pH auf Lateinisch *pondus hydrogenii*.

Wenn sich eine hohe Konzentration von Wasserstoffionen im Wasser befindet, betrachtet man das Wasser als *sauer* (unter 7,0 pH). Wenn sich im Wasser geringe Konzentrationen von Wasserstoffionen befinden, ist es *alkalisch* (mehr als 7,0 pH). Verwesende organische Stoffe (und organische Abfälle) können das Wasser saurer machen. Der neutrale pH-Wert ist 7,0 pH. Für die meisten Aquariumpflanzen liegt der ideale pH-Wert zwischen 6,7 pH und 7,0 pH, weil die meisten Pflanzen aus Gebieten mit saurem Wasser stammen.

Ein weiterer Vorteil eines leicht sauren, bepflanzten Aquariums ist, daß Wasser mit einem pH-Wert unter 7,0 eine höhere Wasserstoffkonzentration hat. Hierdurch wird verursacht, daß mehr ionisches

Ammonium (NH4+), das relativ sicher ist, geformt wird. In Wasser mit einem höheren pH-Wert (alakalisch) wird mehr nicht-ionisches Ammoniak (NH3) geformt, das äußerst giftig ist.

Die Symbole dKH und dH werden weniger verstanden. Selbst viele versierte Hobby-Aquarianer sind sich nicht ganz sicher, welche Unterschiede zwischen dKH und dH bestehen. Ein Teil des Problems liegt darin, daß in der Literatur, in der diese beiden Begriffe beschrieben sind, oft komplexe Terminologie wie *allgemeine Härte, vorübergehende Härte, permanente Härte, GH* und *KH* verwendet wird. Ich werde versuchen, dies zu vermeiden.

Erstens ist kH das Maß der *Karbonathärte*, d.h. der Konzentration von *Karbonaten* und *Bikarbonaten* im Wasser. Ein idealer dKH-Wert liegt bei rund 3 Grad. Der dKH-Wert kann mit Testkits gemessen werden, die im Handel erhältlich sind. Wenn Sie einen Testkit erwerben, achten Sie darauf, daß er die Karbonat- und Bikarbonathärte (dKH) und *nicht* die Kalzium- und Magnesiumhärte (dH) mißt. Falls der dKH-Wert zu niedrig ist, können Sie Leitungswasser hinzufügen (das Karbonathärte hat). Verwenden Si *Natriumhydrogenkarbonat (Backpulver)*, falls Sie den dKH-Wert immer noch erhöhen müssen, aber dies ist normalerweise nur notwendig, wenn Sie destilliertes oder purifiziertes Wasser im Aquarium verwenden.

Normalerweise sind die dKH-Werte eher zu hoch als zu niedrig. Falls der dKH-Wert hoch ist, geben Sie destilliertes Wasser oder Wasser hinzu, das durch *Deionisation und Umkehrosmose* purifiziert wurde. Diese beiden Purifizierungsmethoden werden im nächsten Abschnitt beschrieben. Denken Sie daran, daß der dKH-Wert durch alle Methode verringert wird, mit denen das Wasser enthärtet wird.

Herkömmlicherweise bezieht sich dH auf die *Wasserhärte*, dies ist die Konzentration von Kalziumionen (Ca+) und Magnesiumionen (Mg+) im Wasser. Wenn die Konzentration von Ca+ und Mg+ Ionen im Wasser hoch ist (ist durch einen hohen dH-Wert ersichtlich), wird das Wasser als hartes Wasser angesehen. Niedrige Konzentrationen dieser beiden Ionen (ein niedriger dH-Wert) bedeutet, das Wasser wird als weiches Wasser angesehen.

**Wasserchemie — Wie weiches Wasser erzeugt wird:** In den meisten Fällen steht Hobby-Aquarianern für ihr Aquarium hartes Wasser zur Verfügung, also ist die Erzeugung von hartem Wasser kein Thema. Wenn Sie jedoch hartes Wasser erzeugen müssen, kann das Wasser mit im Handel erhältlichen Chemikalien schnell und einfach „gehärtet" werden. Für die meisten Aquarianer liegt das Hauptproblem darin, *weiches Wasser* zu erzeugen, das niedrige dKH- und dH-Werte hat.

*Regenwasser.* Da sich normalerweise kein Ca+ und Mg+ und keine Bikarbonate im Regen befinden, ist er oft eine ideale Quelle für weiches Wasser. In Industriegebieten sind jedoch hohe Konzentrationen von Schadstoffen wie Schwefeldioxid und Chlorwasserstoff vorhanden, die unvermeidlich in das Regenwasser gelangen.

Falls Sie in einer relativ unverschmutzten Gegend leben, ist Regenwasser eventuell gut für Sie geeignet. Sie sollten jedoch trotzdem etwas *ungechlortes* Leitungswasser hinzufügen, um die richtigen dKH- und dH-Wert zu erhalten.

*Destilliertes Wasser.* Diese Form von Wasser ist die am ehesten erhältliche Form puren Wassers. Es ist sogar ein bißchen *zu* pur; weil destilliertes Wasser praktisch keine Mineralien und nur ein paar aufgelöste Gase enthält, stört es das osmotische Gleichgewicht zwischen dem Wasser und lebenden Organismen.

Das Gleichgewicht wird gestört, weil Mineralien und andere Substanzen aus dem Organismus austreten und in das Wasser gelangen. Die Konzentrationen dieser Mineralien und Substanzen neigen dazu, sich gleichmäßig an der Außenseite und der Innenseite der halbdurchlässigen Membrane des Organismus zu verteilen. Dieser Gleichmäßigkeit kann den Organismus (einschließlich Pflanzen) abtöten. Sollten Sie also destilliertes Wasser verwenden, mischen Sie es mit Leitungswasser, um den gewünschten dKH-Wert zu erhalten. Für ein großes Aquarium ist destilliertes Wasser sehr teuer und keine kostenwirksame Lösung.

*Umkehrosmose.* Das Umkehrosmosegerät erzeugt weiches Wasser—das destilliertem Wasser ähnelt—indem Ionen mit Druck durch eine halbdurchlässige Membrane gegen den osmotischen Gradienten gezwungen werde Vergessen Sie nicht, daß Wasser, das mit einem Umkehrosmosegerät purifiziert wurde, niemals so pur wie destilliertes. Wasser sein wird. Außerdem können die Geräte, die Hobby-Aquarianern normalerweise zur Verfügung stehen, nicht genug Druck erzeugen, um wahrhaft pures Wasser zu produzieren. Sie können jedoch genügend Kalziumionen (Ca+), Magnesiumionen (Mg+) und Bikarbonate entfernen, um das Wasser in bepflanzten Aquarien verwenden zu können.

*Torfmoos.* Torfmoos macht das Wasser weicher, indem es sich mit Ca+ und Mg+ verbindet und gleichzeitig *Tannin* und *Gallinsäure* freigibt. Hierdurch wird der Säuregehalt des Wassers erhöht, was verursacht, daß einige Bikarbonate in $CO_2$ umgewandelt werden, wodurch der dKH-Wert sinkt. Obwohl die Torfmoos-Methode eine der kostenwirksamsten Methoden ist, um das Wasser weicher zu machen, hat sie auch einige Nachteile. Sie geht langsamer als die meisten anderen Methoden vor sich und ist oft nicht genauso gründlich. Sie reduziert den dKH-Wert unter Umständen nicht ausreichend, und das Wasser nimmt außerdem eine gelbliche Farbe an.

Dieser Gelbton des Wassers kann durch die Verwendung von hochwertigem Kohlenstoff in einem mechanischen Filter entfernt werden. Kohlenstoff erhöht jedoch sowohl den dKH-Wert als auch den pH-Wert, weil Karbonate in das Wasser freigegeben werden. Wieviel in das Wasser freigegeben wird, hängt vom Aschegehalt des Kohlenstoffs ab.

**Harz-Enthärtungsmethoden:** Harz wird oft in zwei Methoden eingesetzt, mit denen das Wasser weich gemacht wird — und zwar in der *Natrium-Enthärtungsmethode* und in der *Deionisationsmethode.* Die *Deionisationsmethode* ist der anderen Methode weit überlegen. Die *Natrium-Enthärtungsmethode* ist praktisch nutzlos, wenn man Wasser für Pflanzen weich machen will. Sie ersetzt einfach einen Satz Kationen (Ca+ und Mg+) durch ein anderes Kation (Na+). Viele Leute glauben jedoch irrtümlicherweise, daß das Wasser, so lange es keine Kalzium–und Magnesiumionen enthält, für bepflanzte Aquarien geeignet ist.

*Natrium-Enthärtungsmethode:* Bei dieser Methode wird eine Substanz mit dem Namen *kationischer Harz in Natriumform* kommerziell für die Enthärtung harten Wassers verwendet. Chemisch gesehen entfernt diese Substanz jedoch nicht alle Kationen (wie z.B. Natrium), die ebenfalls zur Härte beitragen, und ihr mangelt es an der Fähigkeit, *Karbonate* oder *Bikarbonate* zu entfernen. Anders gesagt reduziert es den dKH-Wert nicht.

Der Grund dafür, daß diese Methode kommerziell eingesetzt wird, liegt darin, daß auf diese Art enthärtetes Wasser verursacht, daß Seife mehr als in hartem Wasser schäumt und hierdurch die Kosten für Wasser, Seife etc. gesenkt werden.

*Deionisationsmethode:* Diese Methode für die Enthärtung von Aquariumwasser ist besser als die Natriumenthärtungsmethode. In der Deionisation werden zwei Harze verwendet: ein *kationisches Harz in Wasserstoff-Form* (das aus positiv geladenen Ionen besteht) und ein *anionisches Harz in Hydroxylform* (negative Ionen).

Der kationische Harz ersetzt positiv geladene Ionen im Wasser (z.B. Ca+ und Mg+) mit Wasserstoffionen (H+). Ähnlich ersetzt der anionische Harz *Chlorid, Bikarbonate* und *Karbonate* mit dem negativ geladenen Molekül OH-. Ein Nebeneffekt dieses Prozesses ist, daß sich das hierbei entstehenden freie H+ und OH- verbindet und zu Wasser wird ($H_2O$).

Auf diese Art purifiziertes Wasser eliminiert sowohl die Ca+ und Mg+ Härte (dH) als auch die *Karbonathärte* (dKH). Tatsächlich ähnelt das so entstandene Wasser destilliertem Wasser. Genau wie bei destilliertem Wasser müssen Sie auch bei dieser Methode unbedingt Leitungswasser hinzugeben, um den richtigen dKH-Wert zu erhalten.

Außerdem müssen die Harze, nachdem sie mit Chloriden und Karbonaten gesättigt sind, entweder mit einer starken Säure neu aufgeladen oder durch neuen Harz ersetzt werden. Ich rate Ihnen dringend davon ab, das Harz neu aufzuladen. Säure ist extrem gefährlich.

**pH, dKH, dH und $CO_2$:** Die Karbonathärte (dKH), der Säuregehalt und die Menge an Kohlenstoffdioxid im Wasser bestimmen alle zusammen die Gesamtqualität des Wassers. Jeder Faktor beeinflußt die anderen Faktoren. Der pH-Wert Ihres Aquariumwassers hängt von den Niveaus an $CO_2$ und dKH ab. Das CO2 erzeugt Kohlensäure, die den pH-Wert verringert; das dKH (Karbonathärte) fungiert als ein Puffer, der den pH-Wert stabilisiert. Wenn sich der dKH-Wert auf einem idealen Niveau von rund 3 Grad befindet (siehe vorgehende Abschnitte), verhindert er, daß der pH-Wert unter 6,7 pH abfällt, wenn $CO_2$ hinzugefügt wird. Wenn der dKH-Wert zu niedrig ist, sinkt der pH-Wert schon durch eine geringe Menge $CO_2$ unter 6,7 auf ein gefährliches Niveau ab. Ist der dKH-Wert zu hoch, wird die Alkalität (hoher pH-Wert) selbst durch große Mengen $CO_2$ nicht reduziert.

Das dKH-Niveau kann durch Testen des pH-Wertes indirekt ermittelt werden. Wenn CO2 injiziert wird, sollte der pH-Wert prompt sinken. Falls der pH-Wert prompt, aber nicht unter 6,7 absinkt, ist das dKH-Niveau ideal. Falls der pH-Wert unter 6,7 fällt, ist das dKH-Niveau zu niedrig. Umgekehrt ist das dKH-Niveau zu hoch, wenn der pH-Wert nach einer CO2-Injektion nicht prompt auf 6,7 - 7,0 abfällt.

Der dH-Wert wird sich schließlich, wenn Sie den richtigen dKH-Wert (circa 3 Grad) aufrecht erhalten, automatisch in einem akzeptablen Bereich für „weiches Wasser" befinden. Aus diesem Grund habe ich nicht viel Zeit auf dH verwendet. Allen Methode für die Enthärtung des Wassers (durch Kontrolle des dKH-Werts), die vorstehend beschrieben wurden, verringern den dH-Wert ebenfalls. Alle diese Methoden reduzieren sowohl die Konzentration von Bikarbonaten im Wasser (dKH) als auch die Konzentration von Ca+ und Mg+ (dH). Die einzige Ausnahme ist die *Natriumenthärtungsmethode* — sie wird nicht empfohlen.

**Umweltfaktoren und Wasserqualität:** Viele Dekorationen, die Sie eventuell in Ihr Aquarium plazieren wollen (Treibholz, Steine und Kies) können die Qualität und Chemie des Aquariumwassers ändern. Aus bestimmten Steinen und Kies tritt z.B. Kalzium in das Wasser aus, und Treibholz enthält eine Reihe von Chemikalien, die in das Aquarium freigegeben werden. Ich empfehle, Treibholz abzukochen oder lange einzuweichen und Steine und Kies auszuwählen, der weder Kalzium noch Mineralien enthält, durch die die Karbonathärte (dKH) des Wassers erhöht wird.

## Kontrolle von Algen und Schnecken

**Algenkontrolle:** Jedem, der einmal ein Aquarium gehabt hat, sind die mit Algenwachstum verbundenen Frustrationen bekannt. Algen sind nicht nur unattraktiv, sondern sie können auch die Pflanzenrespiration und Photosynthese behindern, indem sie die Blätter der Pflanzen bedecken. Hüten Sie sich besonders vor dem glatten, dunkelgrünen, gelatineähnlichen Film, der blaugrüne Algen genannt wird. Wenn hohe Nitrat-und Phosphat-Niveaus vorhanden sind, wachsen blaugrüne Algen mit einer extrem schnellen Geschwindigkeit und können Pflanzen schnell ersticken. Von allen Algensorten ist dieser Typ am schwersten auszurotten, da es anscheinend keine Fische gibt, die ihn bereitwillig fressen. Es gibt jedoch, so weit ich weiß, ein Produkt, das sowohl blaugrüne Algen als auch andere Algensorten eliminiert: „Health Guard" wird von Seachem Lab hergestellt und kann gefahrlos sowohl mit Fischen als auch mit Pflanzen verwendet werden. Natürlich ist Vorbeugen immer am besten: lassen Sie nicht zu, daß Nitrat und Phosphat derartig so Niveaus in Ihrem Aquarium erreichen.

Wuchernde Algen scheinen besonders in neu eingerichteten Aquarien ein Problem zu sein. Hier ein paar Vorschläge, die Ihnen dabei helfen, die Kontrolle über die Algen in Ihrem Aquarium zu behalten:

(1) Setzen Sie algenfressende Fische wie z.B. *Otocinclus, Epalzeorhynchus siamensis*, Zwerg-Plecostomus oder Fische aus der Familie *Loricariidae* und die meisten Fische der Familie *Poeciliidae* in das Aquarium. Die Arten von Plecostomus, die sehr groß werden, sind jedoch schlecht geeignet, weil viele von ihnen außerdem Pflanzen fressen. Corydoras-Welse können ebenfalls in das Aquarium gesetzt werden, um den Kies aufzuwühlen und zu verhindern, daß sich Algen auf dem Boden des Aquariums ansiedeln. Sie sollten algenfressende Fische hinzugeben, sobald ihr neu eingerichtetes, bepflanztes Aquarium fertig ist. Lassen Sie gar nicht erst zu, daß ein Algenproblem entsteht, bevor Sie die algenfressenden Fische in das Aquarium setzen. Die meisten Fische werden in einem bereits von Algen bewucherten Aquarium nicht viel fressen können und helfen nicht weiter. Geben Sie den Fische wenig Futter, damit sie sich dazu gezwungen sehen, die Algen zu fressen.
(2) Bepflanzen Sie Ihr Aquarium von Anfang an dicht. Achten Sie darauf, daß sie viele schnell wachsenden Pflanzen verwenden. Viele sogenannte „Bündelpflanzen" (Pflanzen, die aus Ablegern gezüchtet und in Bündeln verkauft werden) fallen in diese Kategorie. Rasch wachsende Pflanzen hemmen das Algenwachstum.

(3) Tauschen Sie die Hälfte des Wassers im Aquarium jede Woche (oder *mindestens* alle zwei Wochen) aus, um die stickstoffhaltigen Abfälle und Phosphate zu eliminieren, die zum Gedeihen der Algen beitragen.

(4) Wenn alles andere fehlschlägt, schlagen einige Aquarianer vor, das Aquariumwasser mit einer *sehr schwachen* Kupferlösung zu behandeln, um die Konzentration von Kupfer im Aquarium auf ein Niveau von 0,3 - 0,5 ppm anzuheben. Ich kann gar nicht genug betonen, daß diese Option der *letzte Ausweg* ist. Kupferlösungen, die Algen töten, können sowohl Aquariumpflanzen als auch Fische töten. Tatsächlich ist diese Methode äußerst umstritten. Ich persönlich empfehle diese Methode nicht, aber viele kommerzielle Pflanzenzüchter verwenden Kupferlösungen. Falls Sie *für* diese Methode entscheiden, sollten Sie folgende Tatsachen beachten: ein kleiner Prozentsatz von Pflanzen kann selbst von dieser kleinen Dosis Kupfer getötet werden. Diese „kupferempfindlichen" Pflanzen sind im Informationsbalken für jede Spezies entsprechend markiert. Der Abschnitt *Hinweise für Benutzer* in diesem Buch enthält weitere Informationen zu diesem Thema.

Wenn Sie Kupfer benutzen, müssen Sie es exakt dosieren, weil das Leben Ihrer Pflanzen und Fische hiervon abhängt. Außerdem müssen Sie, wenn Sie fertig sind, entweder das Wasser wechseln oder einen Aktivkohlefilter verwenden, um das Kupfer zu entfernen.

**Schneckenkontrolle:** Die meisten Schnecken können in eiem bepflanzten Aquarium sehr schädlich sein. Zum Beispiel haben Schnecken wie die *Ampullaria paludosa* und die *Marisa rotula* besonders viel Appetit auf Pflanzen. Die *Ampullaria cuprina*, die herkömmlicherweise zur Algenkontrolle verwendet werden, fressen Pflanzen ebenfalls. Grundsätzlich werden die Schnecken im Zaum gehalten, wenn Sie einfach schneckenfressende Fische in das Aquarium setzen, wie z.B. die Süßwasserfische der Gattung *Tetraodon*. Diese Fische haben jedoch den Nachteil, daß sie aggressiv sind, andere Fische im Aquarium beißen und auch oft kleine Fische fressen, wenn sie sie erwischen können. *Botia macracantha* und Zwerg-Botias sind besser geeignet. Ein 6 cm großer *Botia macracantha* kann kleine Schnecken innerhalb von ein paar Tagen problemlos eliminieren.

# Introduction: plantes d'aquarium

Bienvenu dans le monde des plantes d'aquarium! La maintenance d'un aquarium planté peut être un hobby qui vous apporte beaucoup de joie, et malgré tout ce que l'on a pu vous raconter, il n'est pas aussi compliqué. Gardez à l'esprit un certain nombre de règles et vous parviendrez alors à construire votre jardin aquatique pour de nombreuses heures de plaisir et de relaxation.

Nous avons pris soin de limiter à l'extrême le jargon technique. Ainsi, tout le monde se découvrira un "pouce vert."

## La photosynthèse & vos plantes d'aquarium

En installant votre aquarium, ne perdez pas de vue le fait que la photosynthèse est indispensable pour la survie de vos plantes. La photosynthèse est le procédé par lequel les plantes utilisent la chlorophylle et l'énergie lumineuse pour synthétiser l'eau et le gaz carbonique et produire des glucides. Ces glucides permettent aux plantes de se développer.

L'oxygène est primordiale dans la production photosynthétique. Tant que les plantes reçoivent de l'énergie lumineuse, elles absorbent le $CO_2$ contenu dans l'eau et dégagent de l'oxygène dans l'eau. Elles consomment de petites quantités d'oxygène puisqu'elles respirent comme les autres êtres vivants. Toutefois, les quantités consommées sont bien inférieures aux quantités consommées. De même, les quantités de $CO_2$ dégagées sont très inférieures aux quantités d'oxygène.

Pendant les périodes où les plantes n'ont pas de lumière, il n'y a pas de photosynthèse. Cela signifie que les plantes consomment de l'oxygène et dégagent du $CO_2$.

Il est important que le lecteur comprenne bien ce processus et le prenne en compte par la suite. Les chapitres suivants décrivent différentes façons de provoquer la photosynthèse.

### Eclairage naturel ou éclairage artificiel?:
Il vaut mieux placer un aquarium sous un éclairage artificiel plutôt que de le placer sous les rayons du soleil. Cela semble aller contre le sens commun, pourtant, la plupart des plantes ont besoin d'un apport lumineux conséquent, et il est plus facile de contrôler un apport artificiel qu'un apport naturel.

### L'intensité lumineuse:
Chaque variété de plantes demande une intensité lumineuse différente. Toutefois, la cause principale de la mortalité des plantes s'avère être un éclairage pas assez puissant. Aussi, les intensités lumineuses suivantes comportant un spectre lumineux complet sont recommandées pour un aquarium d'une hauteur d'eau de 50 cm:

*Les plantes ayant besoin d'une intensité lumineuse réduite:*
*env. 1.5 – 2.0 watts pour 3.78 litres d'eau.*
*Les plantes ayant besoin d'une intensité lumineuse moyenne:*
*env. 2.5 – 3.0 watts pour 3.78 litres d'eau.*
*Les plantes ayant besoin d'une intensité lumineuse importante:*
*env. 3.5 – 4.0 watts pour 3.78 litres d'eau.*

L'intensité lumineuse diminue fortement lorsque les rayons touchent la surface de l'eau d'un aquarium. Aussi, il est fortement recommandé d'employer des ampoules à vapeur de mercure ou à vapeur de métal pour une hauteur d'eau supérieure à 50 cm. Ces types d'ampoule procurent une intensité lumineuse plus importante que les tubes fluorescent et ceci pour un même wattage.

N'oubliez pas que ces types d'ampoule ont un dégagement de chaleur plus important que les tubes fluorescents. Aussi, il vaut mieux les fixer environ 30 cm au dessus du niveau d'eau. Si vous fermez votre aquarium, pensez à conserver les lampes ou les tubes le plus loin possible de la surface de l'eau et à ventiler cet espace fermé. Sauf si vous utilisez un groupe refroidissant, il est conseillé de ne jamais utiliser des ampoules à vapeur de métal dans un cache fermé.

### Durée d'éclairage:
Je recommande une durée d'éclairage entre 10 et 12 heures. Bien entendu, l'installation d'une minuterie électronique facilite énormément la gestion de l'éclairage. Une programmation de 11 heures à 23 heures par exemple fournira un éclairage suffisant tant que l'intensité lumineuse est suffisante. Cela vous permet également de profiter de votre aquarium pendant la soirée.

### Approvisionnement en $CO_2$:
Comme mentionné auparavant, le dioxyde de carbone ($CO_2$) est indispensable pour que la photosynthèse se produise. Il faut absolument prévoir une fertilisation au $CO_2$ pour conserver ses plantes en bonne santé. Le dioxyde de carbone ($CO_2$) se dissout rapidement dans l'eau et est facilement consommé par les plantes. Aussi, équipez-vous absolument d'un système $CO_2$ pour que vos plantes reçoivent suffisamment de carbone. De nombreux aquariophiles (en particulier aux Etats Unis) pensent que la respiration des poissons dans un aquarium suffit à approvisionner les plantes en $CO_2$. Mais en fait, il faut considérer d'autres aspects. Si vous mettez trop de poissons dans un aquarium, leur respiration peut fournir suffisamment de $CO_2$ pour les plantes, mais vous risquez surtout de ne pas pouvoir gérer cet apport et à terme de provoquer l'asphyxie des poissons.

D'autre part, les poissons produisent des déchets contenant de l'ammoniaque ou des composés azotés. Ces substances sont absorbées par les plantes. Toutefois, si les quantités sont trop importantes, on constate un développement d'algues. En effet, elles aussi trouvent alors suffisamment de nourriture. Un tel développement peut ensuite être nocif pour toute vie dans l'aquarium. Si vous restez sceptique sur les avantages que procure la fertilisation au $CO_2$, observez simplement un aquarium fonctionnant avec ce type de système. Vous constaterez l'apparition de petites bulles d'oxygène sur la surface des plantes. Cela signifie que les plantes effectuent leur travail de photosynthèse. Vous observerez rarement cela dans des aquariums sans ce système. D'autre part, la fertilisation au $CO_2$ permet à l'aquariophile une gestion simple du pH de l'eau de l'aquarium. Les valeurs pH recommandées sont le plus souvent situées entre 6.7 et 7.

### Les taux de $CO_2$:
En règles générales, on injecte environ 8 ppm (parts par million: mg/l) de $CO_2$ dans un aquarium planté. On peut vérifier les quantités injectées à l'aide de tests $CO_2$ ou tout simplement en observant le comportement de certains poissons. Si vous voyez vos poissons haleter, respirer plus rapidement ou aller chercher de l'air à la surface, cela signifie que le taux de $CO_2$ est peut-être trop important. Il est important d'éviter un surdosage, car sinon vous risquez d'asphyxier vos poissons. Les plantes quant à elles n'en seront absolument pas gênées. Aussi, à vous de créer le bon équilibre favorable pour tous les êtres vivant dans votre aquarium. Heureusement, un empoisonnement par dioxyde de carbone est très rare dans un aquarium bien planté.

Si cependant vous constatez un taux excessif de CO2, une forte aération de l'eau résoudra ce problème. Vous pouvez utiliser une pompe à air qui réapprovisionnera l'aquarium en oxygène.

# Introduction: plantes d'aquarium

**L'éclairage et le CO₂:** Pendant les durées d'éclairage, les plantes absorbent plus de $CO_2$ qu'elles n'en produisent. Mais pendant la nuit, elles ne rejettent que du $CO_2$. Aussi, il vaut mieux faire fonctionner son système $CO_2$ uniquement pendant les périodes d'éclairage du bac. N'oubliez donc pas d'arrêter votre système $CO_2$ lorsque les lumières de l'aquarium s'éteignent. Un pH-mètre électronique vous aidera dans cette gestion.

Un bon éclairage sans un apport correct de $CO_2$ne va pas améliorer la photosynthèse. L'inverse, c'est à dire un bon apport de $CO_2$ et un mauvais éclairage réduit également la production photosynthétique. Il faut parvenir à un équilibre entre le taux de $CO_2$ et l'intensité lumineuse.

**Oxygénation pendant la nuit:** Comme pour le $CO_2$, l'oxygénation doit être contrôlée lorsque l'éclairage ne fonctionne pas. Pendant la photosynthèse ( lorsque l'éclairage fonctionne), l'aquarium n'a pas besoin d'être oxygéné puisque les plantes produisent de l'oxygène. Pour faciliter cette gestion, il est conseillé de placer une minuterie sur une pompe à air qui se mettra à fonctionner dès que l'éclairage s'éteindra.

## Température

Les plantes d'aquarium et la plupart des poissons tropicaux vivent dans une eau dont la température varie entre 23 et 28°C. Aussi, il est indispensable dans certaines régions d'équiper son aquarium d'un chauffage ou de le placer dans une pièce chauffée ou, le cas échéant, d'un groupe refroidissant l'eau afin de la maintenir à bonne température. Toutefois, il est recommandé de toujours équiper son aquarium d'un chauffage par le sol, pour provoquer un courant constant vers le haut. Les détails de ce type d'installation vous seront donnés dans le paragraphe concernant *la circulation et le chauffage du substrat*.

Comme un bon éclairage, de bonnes conditions thermiques accélèrent l'activité du métabolisme et la photosynthèse des plantes. Il est donc recommandé d'augmenter les apports lumineux, de $CO_2$ et d'engrais en fonction de la température.

## Les engrais et le substrat

A cause de la décomposition organique, et lorsque vous avez également des poissons, à cause des déjections, l'eau d'un aquarium contient une grande quantité de substances nutritives telles que l'ammonium, les nitrates et les phosphates. Ces substances de base sont les substances principales absorbées par les plantes. Toutefois, seul le potassium (K) n'est pas produit naturellemnt dans l'aquarium. Il faut donc le rajouter.

Un autre groupe de substances nutritives est appelé les oligoéléments. Il comprend le fer (Fe), le cuivre (Cu), le magnésium (Mg), le zinc (Zn), le boron (Br), le sodium (Na), le soufre (S) et le manganèse (Mn). Bien que le potassium ne soit pas vraiment un, on le trouve souvent dans la liste des oligo-éléments de nombreux engrais pour plantes.

**Approvisionnement en oligo-éléments:** Le fer est l'oligo-élément le plus important pour les plantes, parce qu'il rentre dans la composition d'un enzyme permettant la réalisation de la photosynthèse. Sans un apport adéquat, les cellules arrêtent de produire de la chlorophylle et les feuilles deviennent jaunâtre. Et bien entendu, un manque de chlorophylle interrompt la photosynthèse.

On trouve des engrais à base de fer et d'oligo-éléments dans les commerces spécialisés. Ils peuvent être sous forme liquide. On doit alors verser chaque jour quelques gouttes dans l'eau de l'aquarium.

On peut aussi trouver des engrais sous forme de comprimés à placer dans le substrat près des racines des plantes. La fréquence d'utilisation varie selon les produits. Certains additifs liquides permettent à certaines plantes de se nourrir par les feuilles et les tiges.

**Le substrat et les oligo-éléments:** Dans un aquarium planté, le substrat a deux fonctions: il approvisionne en oligo-éléments les racines profondes de certaines plantes, et il empêche ces éléments de s'oxyder. Une oxydation n'est possible qu'en présence d'oxygène. C'est pourquoi il est souvent recommandé de créer des zones anaérobes (pauvres en oxygène) dans l'aquarium. Vos plantes à racines profondes embelliront.

**La circulation et le chauffage du substrat:** Le substrat peut également réchauffer l'eau. Les courants chauds provoquent alors une circulation dans l'aquarium. En effet, les eaux chaudes remontent, tandis que les eaux froides redescendent. Dans le chapitre suivant, *comment installer le substrat*, je recommande l'utilisation d'un cable chauffant qui permet de recréer cette circulation d'eau.

Je n'insisterai jamais assez sur le fait que même si vous vivez dans un pays chaud et que vous refroidissez l'eau avec un groupe-froid, il faut tout de même installer un chauffage créant cette circulation d'eau allant de bas en haut. Si vous refroidissez l'eau de votre aquarium en le laissant dans une pièce avec air conditionné, placez le thermostat du cable chauffant au minimum deux degrés supérieur à la température de la pièce. Ainsi, vous provoquerez le déclenchement du cable chauffant. D'autre part, vous pouvez conserver dans l'aquarium une température supérieure à celle de l'air ambiant de la pièce.

Si vous utilisez un groupe froid, la température de la pièce n'a pas besoin d'être ajustée. Il suffit alors de régler le thermostat du groupe-froid quelques degrés au dessous de la température souhaitée. Une circulation lente de l'eau évite que les déchets azotés ne se déposent par le procédé que je vais décrire maintenant. Tout d'abord, la circulation provoque le passage d'eau dans les couches supérieures du gravier. Cette partie du substrat est une zone aérobe (riche en oxygène) et contient donc des bactéries aérobes. L'ammoniaque que contient l'eau passe dans la zone aérobe et s'oxyde. Grâce aux bactéries, il se transforme alors en nitrites ($NO_2$). Puis, d'autres bactéries transforment les nitrites en nitrates ($NO_3$). Ces deux groupes de bactéries sont appelées des bactéries nitrifiantes.

Certains dénitrateurs ont une influence sur la zone anaérobe (pauvre en oxygène) dont je parlais plus haut. Cette zone doit avoir un petit courant. Les bactéries anaérobes dénitrifiantes de cette zone transforment les nitrates en gaz azoté. Elles agissent en utilisant l'oxygène qu'elles trouvent dans les molécules de nitrates ($NO_3$). Le métabolisme de ces bactéries a besoin d'oxygène comme tous les autres organismes. Quant au gaz azoté, il se dissipe dans l'atmosphère.

**Comment installer le substrat:** Nous allons maintenant vous indiquer comment composer un substrat comportant des zones aérobes et anaérobes.

*1.Le fond:* Poser d'abord le cable chauffant sur le fond de l'aquarium.

*2.La zone anaérobe:* Puis, verser une couche de sable de rivière d'environ 1.5 cm pour recouvrir le cable. Puis, verser un substrat nutritif (en suivant les indications données par le fabricant). Rajouter une autre couche de 1.5 cm de sable de rivière. Ces deux couches forment une zone anaérobe où l'eau s'écoule plus doucement que dans la zone aérobe.

# Introduction: plantes d'aquarium

**3. La zone aérobe:** Puis, ajoutez une couche d'environ 8 cm de sable lavé à larges grains. Cette couche supérieure constitue la zone aérobe, où l'eau s'écoule moins doucement que dans la zone anaérobe. N'oubliez pas qu'il faut continuer de produire un courant grâce au chauffage, car sinon la flore bactérienne anaérobe ne se développera pas, et une zone morte se constituera. D'autre part, cette zone morte va conserver un certain nombre de substances chimiques qui noirciront les racines ou les pourriront.

## Comment installer votre aquarium

Après avoir installé le substrat, vous pouvez commencer à remplir un tiers voire la moitié de l'aquarium. Cela permet d'installer plus facilement les plantes dans l'aquarium. En versant l'eau, prenez garde de ne pas faire remonter le substrat en versant un flot trop important.

Placez une soucoupe ou votre main à l'endroit où vous versez l'eau pour éviter ce problème.

Placez ensuite les plantes en groupes selon leurs variétés, car un éparpillement de plantes n'est pas très joli. Cela reproduira l'aspect qu'elles donnent dans la nature. Lorsque vous avez terminé de planter, vous pouvez finir de remplir l'aquarium.

## Qualité et chimie de l'eau

**Filtration:** La filtration joue plusieurs rôles dans votre aquarium. Tout d'abord, elle vous aide à maintenir l'eau claire. Votre aquarium n'en sera que plus beau. De plus, une eau claire permet à la lumière de pénétrer profondément dans l'aquarium, ce qui est plus important pour la survie des plantes.

Les courants provoqués par la filtration vous permettent de prévenir et de dissiper les dépôts sur les feuilles des plantes. Ces dépôts sont nocifs, car ils bouchent les pores des plantes et les empêchent de respirer. Dans les cas extrêmes, la photosynthèse ne peut plus s'effectuer.

Certains aquariophiles pensent également que le mouvement constant des plantes dans le courant permet de renforcer la structure des plantes.

Il est important de s'assurer que la filtration s'accomplit *sans aération*. J'ai déja expliqué précédemment l'importance du contrôle de l'aération. Le tube de sortie de la filtration doit être bien submergé pour éviter une agitation de l'eau de surface. Ainsi, le CO2 ne s'échappera pas.

La plupart des commerçants proposent des filtres submergeables avec pompe ou des filtres extérieurs que l'on relie à l'aquarium au moyen de tubes. De votre installation va dépendre votre choix. Les filtres extérieurs sont recommandés, lorsque la population en poissons est importante.

**Chimie de l'eau (ou qu'est ce que le pH, le dKH ou la dureté totale?):** La plupart des aquariophiles pensent que le pH est la concentration de l'ion d'hydrogène (H+) dans l'eau. En fait, "pH" signifie potentiel d'hydrogène.

Lorsque l'eau contient une grande concentration d'ions hydrogène, elle est considérée comme acide (en dessous d'un pH7.0). Lorsque l'eau contient une faible concentration d'ions hydrogène, elle est considérée comme alcaline (au dessus d'un pH7.0). Un pH de 7.0 est considéré comme neutre. Les matières en décomposition ou les déchets organiques peuvent acidifier l'eau. Pour la plupart des plantes, le pH idéal est situé entre 6.7 et 7.0. En effet, la plupart des plantes proviennent d'un milieu plutôt acide.

L'avantage de conserver un pH légèrement acide pour les plantes d'aquarium provient du fait que l'eau possède ainsi davantage d'ions d'ammonium positif (NH4+), ce qui n'est pas aussi nocif pour les poissons que lorsque l'eau est alcaline. Car à ce moment on constate une formation d'ammoniaque ce qui est extrêmement toxique.

La dureté totale et la dureté carbonatée sont deux concepts que beaucoup ne comprennent pas très bien. Même certains aquariophiles de grand niveau ne perçoivent pas vraiment la différence entre ces

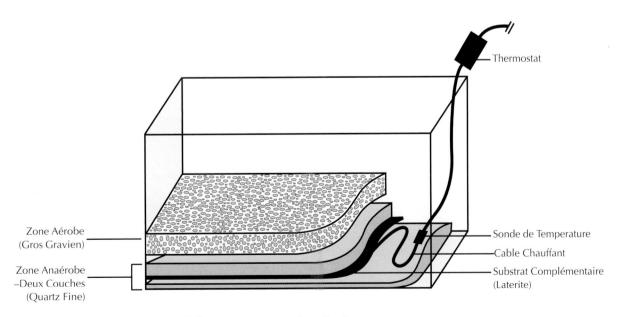

**Diagramme: Le Substrat**

Zone Aérobe
(Gros Gravien)

Zone Anaérobe
–Deux Couches
(Quartz Fine)

Thermostat

Sonde de Temperature

Cable Chauffant

Substrat Complémentaire
(Laterite)

deux duretés. Le problème est que l'on retrouve ces deux concepts sous des appellations très différentes dans la littérature, telles que dureté générale, dureté temporaire, dureté permanente, GH ou KH. Je vais tenter d'éviter ces amalgames.

Le dKH est la mesure de la dureté carbonatée. Il est le taux de carbonates et de bicarbonates dans l'eau. Une valeur dKH idéale est aux environs de 3 degrés. On peut mesurer le dKH à l'aide de tests vendus dans le commerce. Vérifiez bien que ces tests ne mesurent que la dureté carbonatée (dKH) et pas également le calcium et le magnésium (dH).

Si le dKH est trop bas, vous pouvez couper votre eau avec de l'eau du robinet qui a une certaine dureté carbonatée. Vous pouvez aussi employer du bicarbonate de soude (que l'on utilise également pour les sodas) pour augmenter le dKH. Normalement, cela n'est pas nécessaire sauf si vous utilisez de l'eau distillée ou de l'eau purifiée.

Habituellement, les valeurs dKH sont souvent plus élevée que les valeurs souhaitées. Si le dKH est trop élevé, ajoutez de l'eau ayant été purifiée par osmose inverse ou par desioniseur. Ces deux méthodes de purification d'eau sont décrites dans le chapitre suivant. Prenez garde, car toutes les méthodes d'adoucissement de l'eau ne réduisent pas le dKH.

Traditionnellement, le dH se réfère au "degré de dureté" de l'eau et mesure le taux d'ions de calcium (Ca+) et de magnésium (Mg+) dans l'eau. Si le taux d'ions magnésium et d'ions calcium est élevé, l'eau sera dure. L'eau sera douce si les concentrations de calcium et de magnésium sont basses.

*Chimie de l'eau — création d'eau douce:* Dans la plupart des cas, l'eau utilisée par les aquariophiles est dure. Aussi, obtenir une eau dure n'est pas vraiment un problème. Toutefois, si vous deviez durcir votre eau, il existe dans le commerce des produits d'une grande efficacité. Mais le problème principal pour les aquariophiles reste l'obtention d'une eau douce avec des valeurs non élevées de dKH et dH.

*L'eau de pluie:* Parce que l'eau de pluie est normalement exempte de calcium, de magnésium et de bicarbonates, elle est souvent une source idéale d'eau douce. Toutefois, l'emploi d'eau de pluie tombant dans les régions industrialisées où on trouve une forte concentration de produits polluants comme le dioxyde de soufre et le chloride d'hydrogène est fortement déconseillé.

Si vous vivez dans une région non industrielle, l'eau de pluie vous sera d'une grande aide. Vous devrez alors la couper avec de l'eau du robinet ne contenant pas de chlore pour obtenir les bonnes valeurs de dKH et de dH.

*L'eau distillée:* Cette forme d'eau est l'eau pure la plus facile à trouver. Mais en fait, elle s'avère être un peu trop pure, puisqu'elle ne contient aucun minéraux et à peine quelques gaz dissous, ce qui fait qu'elle perturbe la balance osmotique entre l'eau et les organismes vivants.

L'équilibre est instable, car les minéraux et autres substances quittent l'organisme pour aller dans l'eau. Les mêmes concentrations en minéraux et autres substances vont ensuite se répartir équitablement entre l'eau pure et l'organisme en passant par sa menìbrane semi-perméable. Cette répartition peut détruire l'organisme. Aussi, si vous comptez utiliser de l'eau distillée, il vaut mieux la couper avec de l'eau du robinet. Vous obtiendrez plus facilement une bonne valeur dKH. Toutefois, ce procédé est plutôt onéreux quand vous avez un grand aquarium.

*La méthode de l'osmose-inverse:* Les osmoseurs fournissent une eau adoucie aux qualités proches de l'eau distillée. Ils fonctionnent en envoyant les ions à grande pression au travers d'une membrane semi-

perméable agissant ainsi avec un principe inverse à l'osmose. Bien sûr, l'eau osmosée ne peut jamais devenir aussi pure que l'eau distillée. Les osmoseurs accessibles dans le commerce ne fonctionnent pas sous une pression suffisante pour en fabriquer. Mais ces appareils fournissent une eau que l'on peut verser directement dans l'aquarium, puisqu'ils enlèvent des quantités suffisantes d'ions calcium (Ca+), d'ions magnésium (Mg+) et de bicarbonates.

*La filtration sur tourbe:* La filtration sur tourbe adoucit l'eau en liant les ions calcium et les ions magnésium et en libérant de l'acide tannique et de l'acide gallique. Elle acidifie l'eau, ce qui transforme certains bicarbonates en $CO_2$ et baisse les valeurs dKH. Bien que cette méthode soit la moins chère, elle présente tout de même plusieurs inconvénients. Elle prend bien plus de temps et n'est souvent pas aussi efficace que les autres méthodes. De plus, les valeurs dKH ne baissent pas suffisamment, et l'eau de l'aquarium prend une coloration jaune.

On peut éliminer cette coloration en mettant du charbon actif dans un filtre mécanique. Le charbon augmente le dKH et le pH en libérant des carbonates dans l'eau. La quantité de carbonates libérés dépend de la cendre contenue dans le charbon.

**Les résines adoucissantes:** On emploie des résines pour adoucir l'eau dans deux méthodes: la méthode d'adoucissement au sodium et la méthode de déminéralisation.

La méthode d'adoucissement au sodium est souvent inutile lorsque l'on veut adoucir l'eau pour les plantes. Elle se contente de remplacer certains cations (Ca+ et Mg+) par d'autres (Na+).

Toutefois, de nombreuses personnes pensent à tort que si l'eau ne contient pas de calcium et de magnésium, elle est bonne pour les plantes.

*La méthode d'adoucissement au sodium:* On utilise dans ce procédé une substance appelée "résine cationique sous forme de sodium" qui adoucit l'eau dure. Cependant, chimiquement parlant, cette substance n'enlève pas tous les cations (comme le sodium) qui contribuent aussi à la dureté et elle n'a pas la capacité d'enlever les bicarbonates et les carbonates. En d'autres mots, elle ne baisse pas le dKH.

Commercialement, on préfère utiliser cette méthode, car l'eau adoucie de cette manière n'a pas besoin de quantités de conditionneurs d'eau aussi importantes qu'avec une eau dure, ce qui réduit considérablement les frais.

*La méthode de déminéralisation:* Cette méthode d'adoucissement d'eau est meilleure que la méthode précédente. Deux résines sont employées lors de la déminéralisation: une résine cationique sous forme hydrogène (contenant des ions positifs) et une résine anionique sous forme hydroxyle (contenant des ions négatifs).

La résine cationique lie dans l'eau des ions chargés positivement (comme Ca+ ou Ma+) à des ions hydrogènes (H+). En outre, la résine anionique lie les chlorides, les bicarbonates et les carbonates à la molécule OH- chargée négativement. Cette méthode a un effet secondaire: l'H+ et l'OH- qui se libèrent, se lient et se transforme en eau.

L'eau purifiée de cette manière élimine la dureté totale dH (Ca+ et Mg+)et la dureté carbonatée dKH. En fait, le résultat obtenu est similaire à l'eau distillée. Comme pour l'eau distillée, il vous faut couper votre eau avec de l'eau du robinet pour obtenir le bon dKH.

Dès que ces résines sont saturées de chlorides et de carbonates, elles ont besoin d'être rechargées avec un acide très puissant ou d'être remplacées. Attention, car l'acide est très dangereux.

# Introduction: plantes d'aquarium

**PH, dKH, dH et CO$_2$:** La dureté carbonatée (dKH), l'acidité et le taux de dioxyde de carbone (CO$_2$), tous ces éléments contribuent à mesurer la qualité moyenne de l'eau. Chaque paramètre affecte les autres. Le pH de l'eau est déterminé par le taux de CO$_2$ et le dKH. Le CO$_2$ génère de l'acide carbonique qui diminue le pH. Quant au dKH, il a une capacité tampon qui stabilise les valeurs pH. Si les valeurs dKH sont bonnes (3°, voir les chapitres précédents), elles évitent que le pH ne passe en dessous de 6.7 lorsque l'on rajoute du CO$_2$. Mais lorsque le dKH est trop bas, une faible quantité de CO$_2$ sera capable de faire chuter le pH en dessous de 6.7, c'est à dire à une valeur dangereuse pour l'aquarium. Si le dKH est trop haut, même de grandes quantités de CO$_2$ ne parviendront pas à réduire l'alcalinité de l'eau (le pH sera élevé).

Le niveau du dKH peut être déterminé indirectement avec un test pH. Lorsque le CO$_2$ est injecté, le pH devrait chuter facilement. Si le pH chute facilement, mais ne passe pas en dessous de la valeur 6.7, le dKH est idéal. Si le pH passe en dessous de 6.7, le dKH est trop bas. A l'inverse, si le fait d'injecter du CO$_2$ ne baisse pas le pH jusqu'aux valeurs souhaitées (6.7–7.0), cela signifie que le dKH est trop élevé.

En fait, si vous parvenez à maintenir un bon dKH, le dH chutera automatiquement pour donner des valeurs correctes pour une eau douce.

C'est pour cette raison que je n'ai pas expliqué le dH en détail. Toutes les méthodes d'adoucissement de l'eau décrites ci-dessus, à l'exception de l'adoucissement au sodium, diminuent le dH en contrôlant le dKH. Elles réduisent en même temps le taux de bicarbonates (dKH) et la concentration en Ca+ et en Mg+ (dH).

**Facteurs environnementaux & qualité de l'eau:** Lorsque l'on décide de décorer son aquarium, il faut savoir que de nombreuses décorations ( comme les racines, les pierres ou le sable…) peuvent modifier la qualité et la chimie de l'eau. Par exemple, certaines pierres ou certains graviers peuvent libérer du calcium dans l'eau, tandis que certaines racines peuvent laisser échapper des substances chimiques. Il vaut mieux faire bouillir les racines ou bien les laisser tremper avant de les placer dans l'aquarium, et n'utiliser que des roches ou du sable ne libérant ni calcium, ni minéraux pour éviter une augmentation de la dureté carbonatée (dKH).

## Le contrôle du développement d'algues et d'escargots.

**Le contrôle du développement des algues:** Toute personne s'étant occupé d'un aquarium a été confronté au problème de la croissance des algues. Les algues ne sont pas seulement inesthétiques, elles peuvent également empêcher la respiration des plantes en recouvrant la surface de leurs feuilles et donc interrompre la photosynthèse. En particulier, il faut prendre garde au film lisse, de couleur vert foncé, d'aspect gélatineux que l'on nomme les algues vertes.

Ces algues ont une croissance extrêmement rapide lorsque l'eau contient de grandes quantités de nitrates et de phosphates. Elles peuvent s'étendre très rapidement. De toutes les algues, ce type s'avère être le plus difficile à éradiquer, car on ne trouve pas de poissons qui s'en nourrissent facilement. Toutefois, il existe certains produits dans le commerce qui les éliminent sans être nocifs pour les poissons et les plantes. Bien entendu, la meilleure approche est de prévoir ces développements intempestifs. Il suffit alors d'éviter que les taux de nitrates et de phosphates ne dépassent les valeurs moyennes.

La croissance des algues rampantes semble être un problème typique pour les aquariums que l'on vient d'installer. Mais vous trouverez ci-dessous quelques suggestions qui vous aideront à contrôler la croissance des algues:

(1) Introduisez des poissons mangeurs d'algues comme les *Otocinclus*, les *Epalzeorhynchus siamensis*, les *Plecostomus* nains, certains poissons-chats ou d'autres poissons mangeurs d'algues de la famille des *Loricariidés* ou des ovipares de la famille des *Poecilia*. Toutefois, le choix de types de *Plecostomus* qui deviennent grand est déconseillé, car ils mangent également les plantes. Les *Corydoras* peuvent aussi être introduits, car ils cherchent leur nourriture dans le gravier et empêchent alors les algues de s'implanter sur le substrat.

Pour éviter tout problème, introduisez les poissons mangeurs d'algues au plus tôt. Vous résoudrez ainsi les problèmes à la base. La plupart des poissons ne seront pas capable de manger suffisamment d'algues dans un aquarium déjà envahi. Ne nourrissez pas trop vos poissons, sinon ils risquent de ne plus avoir assez faim pour s'attaquer aux algues.

(2) Dès le départ, placez une grande quantité de plantes. Assurez-vous d'inclure un grand nombre de plantes à croissance rapide. De nombreuses plantes, des boutures vendues en bouquet, font partie de ces plantes à croissance rapide. Ce type de plantes empêche la croissance des algues.

(3) Changez chaque semaine la moitié de l'eau de l'aquarium pour enlever les déchets azotés et les phosphates qui provoquent la croissance des algues.

(4) Si tous les conseils donnés ci-dessus ne vous aident pas, certains aquariophiles suggèrent de traiter l'eau de l'aquarium avec de petites quantités de cuivre. L'eau de l'aquarium doit obtenir un taux de cuivre entre 0.3 et 0.5 ppm (mg/l). Je ne soulignerai jamais assez le fait que je considère cette solution comme une solution de dernière chance. En effet, les solutions à base de cuivre peuvent tuer les algues, mais elles peuvent également tuer les plantes et les poissons. En fait, cette méthode est extrêmement controversée. C'est pour cette raison que je ne la recommande pas bien que de nombreux cultivateurs de plantes l'emploient.

Si vous souhaitez tout de même procéder de cette façon, prenez garde aux points suivants: un petit pourcentage de plantes peut être tué par des quantités même très petites de cuivre. Ces plantes plus fragiles sont indiquées dans les barres d'information de chaque variété. Vous trouverez de plus amples informations dans le guide de l'utilisateur de ce livre. Prenez des mesures très précises lorsque vous utilisez du cuivre. La vie de vos plantes et de vos poissons en dépend. De même, après un traitement, assurez-vous que vous avez bien changé une partie de l'eau ou filtrez votre eau au charbon actif pour enlever le cuivre.

**Le contrôle de la croissance des escargots:** La plupart des escargots peuvent avoir une action destructive sur les plantes d'un aquarium. Les *Ampullaria paludosa* et les *Marisa rotula* en sont particulièrement voraces. Les *Ampullaria cuprina* qui sont particulièrement employés contre les algues, mangent également les plantes. Le procédé le plus efficace pour éviter toute prolifération est de rajouter des poissons mangeurs d'escargots. Cela inclue les poissons-globe d'eau douce. L'introduction de ce type de poissons a un revers: ils sont très aggressifs. Ils mordent les autres poissons de l'aquarium et mangeront les petits poissons qu'ils pourront attraper. Il vaut mieux choisir les *Botias macracantha* et les *Botias* nains. D'autre part, un de 6 cm peut facilement éliminer les petits escargots en quelques jours.

# Inleiding Tot Aquariumplanten

Welkom in de wereld van de aquariumplanten. Een aangeplant aquarium houden kan een dankbare hobby zijn die — ondanks al wat u erover hebt gehoord - helemaal niet moeilijk is. Hou in het achterhoofd enkele eenvoudige regels en feiten en u zal goed en wel op weg zijn naar een degelijk gedijende onderwatertuin die voor heel wat uren van schoonheid en ontspanning zal zorgen.

De gegeven informatie is eenvoudig en we hebben het technische jargon tot een minimum beperkt. Zoals u zal zien, in principe kan iedereen beschikken over een "groene onderwatertuin."

## Fotosynthese En Uw Aquariumplanten

Bij het opzetten van uw aquarium moet u goed onthouden hoe belangrijk fotosynthese is om planten gezond te houden. Fotosynthese is een proces waarbij planten chlorofyl gebruiken om met behulp van lichtenergie de omzetting te doen van water, kool (te vinden in kooldioxide of andere kool-samenstellingen) en verscheidene andere voedingsstoffen naar eenvoudige suikers. Deze suikers dienen voor de groei en het instandhouden van de planten.

Een belangrijker nevenproduct van fotosynthese is zuurstof. Om dat te doen halen planten tijdens perioden van licht, de kooldioxide ($CO_2$) uit het water en geven ze zuurstof af. Maar, net als dieren, ademen planten constant: ze halen zuurstof uit het water en geven $CO_2$ af in hun omgeving. Tijdens de perioden van licht (wanneer fotosynthese optreedt) is de opgenomen hoeveelheid zuurstof minimaal, vergeleken met de hoeveelheid die door de plant terzelfdertijd wordt vrijgegeven. Evenzo is de hoeveelheid vrijgegeven $CO_2$ onbetekenend in vergelijking met de afgegeven zuurstof.

Tijdens donkere perioden valt fotosynthese weg. Dat betekent dat, wanneer de plant ademt, zij zuurstof opneemt en $CO_2$ afgeeft. Het is voor de hobbyist belangrijk op de hoogte te zijn van deze processen en die in acht te nemen bij het opzetten van een aquarium. Volgende paragrafen beschrijven eenvoudige middelen om daaraan tegemoet te komen.

**Belichting: natuurlijk- versus kunstlicht:** Het is een goed idee om een beplant aquarium weg te houden van een natuurlijke lichtbron zoals zonlicht en liever te vertrouwen op kunstlicht. Dit schijnt in te gaan tegen een gangbare mening, maar onthou dat planten per dag een vrij behoorlijke hoeveelheid licht nodig hebben en sommige onder hen om een bepaalde lichtintensiteit vragen. Aan deze eisen is moeilijk te voldoen met natuurlijk licht maar ze zijn integendeel gemakkelijk te bereiken met kunstlicht.

**Lichtintensiteit:** Niet alle planten vragen om dezelfde lichthoeveelheid. Onaangepaste verlichting (meestal te weinig) is de meest voorkomende oorzaak van afstervende aquariumplanten. Volgende aanbevelingen gelden voor een aquarium tot 50 cm hoog en bij gebruik van een full-spectrum fluorescerend licht. Planten die :

*gedempte verlichting vereisen: ong. 1.5…2 Watt per 3.78 l.*
*matige verlichting vereisen: ong. 2.5…3 Watt per 3.78 l.*
*heldere verlichting vereisen: ong. 3.5…4.5 Watt per 3.78 l.*

De lichtintensiteit neemt wezenlijk af op de bodem van het aquarium. Om die reden raad ik halogeen- of kwikdamplampen aan voor een aquarium van meer dan 50 cm hoog. Ze geven meer licht dan fluorescentiebuizen van hetzelfde vermogen (uitgedrukt in Watt). Vergeet niet dat dergelijke halogeen- of kwikdamplampen heel wat warmer worden dan fluorescentiebuizen. U moet ze dus ophangen op zowat 30 cm boven een open, niet afgedekt aquarium. Gebruikt u een afdekkap, hou dan de lichten (zelfs fluorescentiebuizen) zo ver mogelijk verwijderd van het wateroppervlak en voorzie voldoende ventilatie onder de kap. Monteer nooit halogeenlampen, tenzij u beschikt over een koel-eenheid, aan de binnenzijde van een kap.

**Lichtduur:** Ik raad een lichtperiode aan van 10…12 uur. Een comfortoplossing daarbij is een automatische timer. Wanneer u die timer instelt op "licht" tussen ongeveer 11.00 en 23.00 uur dan voorziet u de planten van voldoende licht en laat dit u toe om tijdens de avonduren te genieten van uw aquarium.

**Toevoer van kooldioxide:** Zoals reeds vroeger vermeld is koolzuur een onmisbaar deel van de fotosynthese en moet dus aanwezig zijn om aquariumplanten gezond te houden. Kooldioxide ($CO_2$) lost snel op in water en is de eenvoudigste koolcomponente die planten kunnen gebruiken. Ik kan u een $CO_2$ injectiesysteem aanraden om aquariumplanten van voldoende koolzuur te voorzien.

Veel aquarianen (vooral in de VS) geloven dat in een aquarium met planten en vissen, het ademhalen van de vissen volstaat als $CO_2$-bron voor de planten. Er is echter méér. Indien u van plan bent om een extreem dichte vispopulatie in het aquarium te houden, dan kan hun ademhaling wel voldoende $CO_2$ produceren maar, de (negatieve) gevolgen van de overbevolking in het aquarium nemen elk voordeel weg. Vissen zijn dieren en dieren produceren afval. Een grote vispopulatie produceert derhalve immense hoeveelheden ammoniak en stikstof-componenten. Beide zijn bruikbaar voor de planten maar een teveel ervan kan oorzaak zijn van een niet te controleren algenbloei.

Mocht u nog altijd sceptisch staan tegenover het voordeel van een $CO_2$ injectiesysteem, kijk dan even naar een aquarium waar er een is geinstalleerd. U zal kleine zuurstofbelletjes merken die opstijgen van uit de planten, wat meteen aanduidt dat een gezonde fotosynthese in werking is. Dat zal u zelden opmerken in een aquarium zonder een dergelijk systeem.

Bovenop de functie van koolzuurtoevoer voor de planten kan een $CO_2$ injectiesysteem door hobbyisten ook gebruikt worden om in het aquarium het vereiste pH-niveau (meestal tussen de 6.7 en 7.2) te onderhouden. Kooldioxide niveau:

In het algemeen ligt een goed $CO_2$ peil om en bij de 8 deeltjes per miljoen (ppm). Dit kan worden nagegaan met een kooldioxide testkit of gewoon door het observeren van het gedrag van de vissen in het aquarium. Als u de vissen ziet hijgen of snel ademen of wanneer ze aan de oppervlakte zwemmen om naar adem te happen, dan is het $CO_2$ gehalte te hoog.

**Onthou:** al is kooldioxide goed voor de planten, overdreven hoeveelheden kunnen de vissen doden! U moet immers tegemoet komen aan de noden van alle aquariumbewoners. Gelukkig komt $CO_2$ vergiftiging niet veel voor in een beplant aquarium.

Mocht het $CO_2$ peil in uw aquarium te hoog worden, dan zal een hevige beluchting van het water het probleem dadelijk oplossen. Door het aquarium met een zuurstofpomp te beluchten zorgt u dat het $CO_2$ ontsnapt en vervangen wordt door zuurstof.

**Licht en $CO_2$:** Herinner u dat gedurende perioden van licht de planten meer $CO_2$ uit het water halen dan ze erin vrijgeven: gedurende donkere perioden echter laten ze meer $CO_2$ vrij. Daarom moeten licht en $CO_2$ systeem samenwerken. Wanneer het licht aan is moet de $CO_2$ injectie eveneens werken. Bij het uitschakelen van de verlichting mag u niet vergeten om ook de kooldioxide injectie uit te schakelen. Door onvoldoende $CO_2$ bij normaal licht zal het effect van de fotosynthese die aan de gang is verminderen. Daartegenover staat dat bij het toevoegen van kooldioxide zonder voldoende licht (waarbij de fotosynthese klein wordt), er een teveel aan $CO_2$ in het water ontstaat.

Er moet dus een evenwicht bestaan tussen lichtniveau en de hoeveelheid $CO_2$ die wordt geinjecteerd om een goede werking van de fotosynthese te bereiken.

**Nachtbeluchting:** Net zoals $CO_2$ moet de beluchting in functie van het licht worden gecontroleerd. Tijdens de fotosyntheseperiode (lichten aan) moet het aquarium niet belucht worden. Beluchting (zoals eerder besproken) zorgt ervoor dat $CO_2$ uit het water ontsnapt. Dit is nodig tijdens de nachtelijke periode wanneer planten enkel ademen (zuurstof opnemen en kooldioxide uitstoten). Een eenvoudige manier om zeker te zijn dat beluchting en lichtcyclus gepast op elkaar inwerken bestaat er in om de luchtpomp te verbinden met een timer die tegengesteld aan die van de lichten is geprogrammeerd.

## Temperatuur

Aquariumplanten en de meeste tropische vissen vragen om een temperatuur van ongeveer 23 tot 28° C. Hobbyisten die wonen in gebieden met extreme temperatuursvariaties doorheen het jaar moeten investeren in een apparatuur die het water van hun aquarium rond deze waarden houdt.

In streken waar tijdens bepaalde seizoenen de temperatuur onder de 20° C daalt is het nodig om uw aquarium in een verwarmd lokaal te houden of die te voorzien van een verwarmingselement. In gebieden waar de temperatuur de 32 °C overschrijdt kan u het aquarium opstellen in een luchtgekoelde (airco) kamer of - en dat is een betere oplossing - een koeler in het aquarium plaatsen.

Hoedanook, zelfs in streken waar het nodig is om het water te koelen (via airco of koeler), is een verwarmingselement onder de bodembedekking van uw aquarium aan te bevelen om een verticale watercirculatie op te wekken. Details dienaangaande worden besproken in de paragraaf: circulatie en verwarming van de bodembedekking.

Tenslotte, net zoals bij een sterkere belichting, zal stijgende temperatuur de stofwisselingen en de fotosynthese versnellen. Het ware dus verstandig om lichtwaarde, CO2 en voedingsstoffen evenredig met de temperatuur te verhogen.

## Voedingsstoffen En De Bodembedekking

Door de ontbinding van organisch materiaal en (indien in uw beplant aquarium vissen leven) dierlijke afvalstoffen, bevatten aquaria meestal een overtollige hoeveelheid aan voedingsstoffen zoals ammoniak, nitraten en fosfaten. Deze fundamentele, overvloedig aanwezige bestanddelen zijn de belangrijkste voedingselementen voor aquariumplanten. Onder deze hoofdbestanddelen wordt enkel Kalium (K) niet op een natuurlijke wijze aangemaakt in uw aquarium en zal dus moeten toegevoegd worden.

Een andere belangrijke groep van voedingselementen noemen we microvoedingsstoffen. Ze omvatten ijzer(Fe), koper(Cu), magnesium (Mg), zink (Zn), Broom (Br), Natrium (Na), Zwavel (S) en Mangaan(Mn). Alhoewel Kalium geen eigenlijke microvoedingsstof is

wordt het toch toegevoegd aan heel wat producten van microvoedingsadditieven voor planten.

**Toevoegen van microvoedingsstoffen:** IJzer is een der meest noodzakelijke microvoedingsstoffen omdat het een component is van het enzym dat fotosynthese ondersteunt. Zonder voldoende ijzer stopt de cel de productie van chlorofyl en de bladeren krijgen een ziekelijke gele kleur. Bovendien is het onmogelijk om zonder chlorofyl te komen tot een voldoende fotosynthese voor een goede groei van de planten.

IJzerbemesting is verkrijgbaar bij de dealers zoals andere bemestingen die al de noodzakelijke microvoedingsstoffen bevatten. Voeibare bemestingen moeten één- of tweemaal per week worden toegevoegd. Wanneer u bemesting in tabletvorm gebruikt moet u die plaatsen in het grind naast de wortels van de bedoelde plant. De bijsluiter vermeldt hoe vaak u een nieuwe tablet moet plaatsen.

Door om de week vloeibare microvoedingsbemesting aan het water toe te voegen kunnen de planten - in het bijzonder de gedeeltelijk gewortelde en de wortelloze planten - de gepaste hoeveelheden van deze voedingsstoffen via bladeren en stengels absorberen.

**Bodembedekking en microvoedingsstoffen:** In een beplant aquarium heeft de bodembedekking twee functies: zij voorziet de diep gewortelde planten van een continue toevoer van microvoedingsstoffen en voorkomt dat diezelfde stoffen oxideren. Daarom is het belangrijk om een anaërobe (zuurstofarm) zone in uw aquarium te creëren, dit in het voordeel van diepgewortelde planten.

**Circulatie en bodemverwarming:** De bodembedekking kan het water opwarmen en aldus de circulatie in het aquarium bevorderen. In de volgende paragraaf (hoe de bodembedekking samenstellen) geef ik de raad een verwarmingskabel te leggen op de bodemplaat. De warmte van de kabel veroorzaakt een trage vertikale (van onder naar boven) waterverplaatsing. Deze waterverplaatsing is het gevolg van het feit dat warm water stijgt en koud water daalt. De circulatie in het aquarium wordt dus onderhouden door het stijgen van warme moleculen en het dalen van koude.

Ik kan niet genoeg het feit benadrukken dat, ook al woont u in een warme streek waar u het aquariumwater moet koelen, u toch een verwarming nodig hebt onder de bodembedekking omdat uw aquarium een vertikale circulatie nodig heeft. Indien u het water koelt door het aquarium te plaatsen in een gekoelde ruimte, zet dan de thermostaat van de verwarmingskabel minimum een tweetal graden boven de kamertemperatuur. Dat heeft voor gevolg dat de verwarmingskabel de circulatie zal activeren. Dus, de temperatuur in het lokaal moet lager liggen dan de temperatuur in uw aquarium.

Indien u een koeler gebruikt dan moet de kamertemperatuur niet noodzakelijk worden aangepast. Zet gewoon de thermostaat verscheidene graden hoger dan de beoogde temperatuur van het aquariumwater.

Een vlotte watercirculatie in het aquarium helpt de aangroei van stikstofhoudend afval tegengaan via een proces dat ik nu wil beschrijven. Vooreerst veroorzaakt de watercirculatie een constante vloed doorheen de bovenste laag van de bodembedekking die is samengesteld uit doorlatend grind. Deze bovenlaag is een "aërobe zone," wat betekent: zuurstofrijk. Deze zone bevat aërobe bacteriën. De ammoniak in het water dat door deze doorlaatbare bovenlaag vloeit wordt door de bacteriën geoxideerd tot nitriet ($NO_2$). Dit nitriet wordt dan door andere bacteriën omgevormd tot nitraat ($NO_3$). Toepasselijk worden deze twee groepen bacteriën "nitrificerende bacteriën" genoemd.

# Inleiding Tot Aquariumplanten

Sommige nitraatfilters horen thuis onderaan in de "anaërobe (zuurstofarm) zone. Doorheen deze zone mag slechts een zwakke waterstroom vloeien. De anaerobe bacteriën in deze zone vormen het $NO_3$ om tot nitraatgas. De bacterie doet dat door gebruik te maken van de zuurstof in het $NO_3$ want zoals in elk organisme is er zuurstof nodig voor de stofwisseling die door deze bacterie wordt bewerkt. Het ontstane nitraatgas komt vrij in de atmosfeer.

**Hoe een bodembedekking uitbouwen:** Wat volgt is een leiddraad bij het uitbouwen van een bodembedekking met verwarming, aërobe en anaërobe zones.

**(1) De bodem:** Leg een verwarmingskabel op de bodem van het aquarium in zig-zag vorm.

**(2) De anaërobe zone:** Strijk boven de verwarmingskabel een zowat 1.5 cm dikke laag fijn riviergrind uit (grover dan siliciumzand) en strooi bovenop deze drager substraat additieven (volg daarbij de gebruiksaanwijzing). Hierboven komt dan nog een laag van 1.5 cm fijn riviergrind. Beide lagen vormen een anaërobe zone waardoorheen het water trager vloeit dan in de aërobe zone.

**(3) De aërobe zone:** Vervolledig tenslotte met ongeveer 8 cm gewassen grofkorrelig grind van 2…3 mm. Deze bovenlaag is de aërobe zone waardoorheen het water gemakkelijker stroomt dan doorheen de anaërobe zone eronder. Onthou dat er een opwaartse stroom moet bestaan (veroorzaakt door het verwarmingselement), zoniet zullen de anaërobe bacteriën in het onderste gedeelte van de bodembedekking niet kunnen functioneren en aldus een zgn. "dode zone" doen ontstaan. Meer nog, deze dode zone wordt een verzamelpunt van chemische bestanddelen die de wortels doen rotten en zwart worden.

## Het Opzetten Van Uw Aquarium

Na het samenstellen van de bodembedekking kan u het aquarium voor $\frac{1}{3}$ tot $\frac{1}{2}$ opvullen. Dit vergemakkelijkt het aanplanten. Bij het vullen van het aquarium mag u de bodembedekking niet verstoren door er het water ongeremd overheen te gieten.

Een middel om dit te vermijden is een bord of uw hand te gebruiken om de waterstroom te breken zodat het water zachtjes in het aquarium kan vloeien.

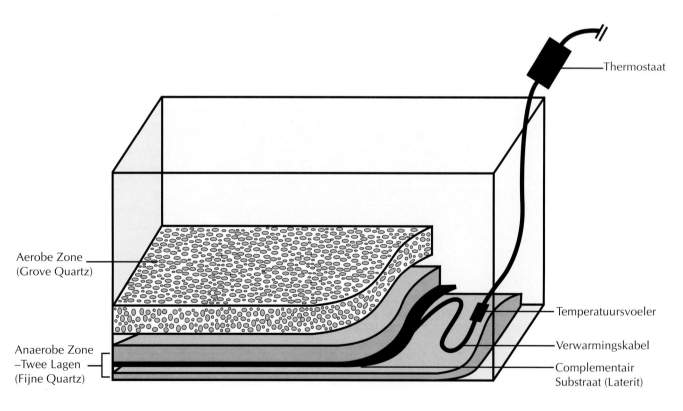

Aerobe Zone
(Grove Quartz)

Anaerobe Zone
–Twee Lagen
(Fijne Quartz)

Thermostaat

Temperatuursvoeler

Verwarmingskabel

Complementair
Substraat (Laterit)

**Diagram: Het Substraat**

# Inleiding Tot Aquariumplanten

Eenmaal het aquarium gedeeltelijk gevuld kan u met aanplanten beginnen. Groepeer elke soort op een welbepaalde plaats, liever dan ze over heel het aquarium te verdelen. Dit zal een betere weergave zijn van de natuurlijke groei van de planten. Na het aanplanten kan u het aquarium volledig vullen.

## WATERKWALITEIT EN CHEMIE

**Filtering:** het filter vervult in uw aquarium enkele belangrijke functies. Vooreerst helpt het de helderheid van het water bevorderen. Helder water is niet alleen aantrekkelijker dan troebel water, het zorgt ervoor dat het licht, en dat is belangrijker, tot op de bodem van het aquarium kan doordringen.

Twee: De waterstroom door het filter veroorzaakt, belet dat resten zich afzetten op de bladeren van de planten. Deze resten zijn vaak schadelijk omdat het de bladporiën (de stomata) dichtslibt en aldus de plant belet om te ademen. In het extreme geval kan een aaneenkitten van dit slib de fotosynthese verhinderen.

Drie: Veel aquarianen geloven dat de constante beweging der planten veroorzaakt door het stromende water, hun structuur helpt verstevigen. Vergewis er u van dat filtering in uw aquarium gbeurt zonder beluchting (ik besprak in wat voorafging de noodzaak om deze beluchting in de hand te houden). De uitgang van de filterapparatuur moet vrij ver onder het wateroppervlak gelegen zijn om te voorkomen dat de bovenste waterlagen beroerd worden wat meteen zou inhouden dat een groot verlies aan $CO_2$ ontstaat.

De meeste vakhandelaars bieden zowel binnen-als buitenfilters aan. Uw keuze zal worden bepaald door uw aquariumontwerp waarbij uitwendige filters geschikt zijn voor een dichtbevolkt aquarium.

**Waterchemie — (wat is pH, dKH en dH?):** Voor de meeste hobbyisten betekent pH de concentratie aan waterstofionen (H+) in het water. Inderdaad, pH staat in het latijn voor "kracht van waterstof."

Water met een hoge concentratie waterstofionen wordt aanzien als zuur (pH onder de 7.0). Bij en kleinere concentratie is het water alkalisch (pH boven de 7.0). Rottend organisch materiaal evenals organisch afval kan het water zuur maken. De waarde 7.0 wordt als een neutrale pH aanzien. Voor de meerderheid der aquariumplanten ligt een ideale pH tussen 6.7 en 7.0 omdat de meeste onder hen afkomstig zijn uit regionen met een eerder zure wateromgeving.

Voor een aangeplant aquarium is een licht-zure wateromgeving met een pH-waarde onder de 7.0 een bijkomend voordeel omdat die waarde een hogere concentratie aan waterstof betekent. Dit resulteert in de vorming van meer ammoniakionen (NH4+), meteen een bijkomende veiligheidsfactor gezien in alkalisch water (hogere pH) meer niet-ionisch ammoniak wordt gevormd en dat laatste is erg giftig.

Minder bekend is dKH en dH. Zelfs heel wat ervaren hobbyisten zijn niet helemaal zeker van het verschil tussen die twee. Oorzaak van het probleem is, dat de literatuur die deze twee beschrijft dikwijls ingewikkelde bewoordingen gebruikt zoals bv. "algemene hardheid," "tijdelijke hardheid," "blijvende hardheid," "GH" en "KH." Ik zal proberen om dat te vermijden.

Om te beginnen, dKH is een maat voor de carbonaat hardheid. Dat wijst op de concentratie aan carbonaten en bicarbonaten in het water. Een ideale waarde ligt rond de 3 graden. Deze dKH-waarde kan worden gemeten met testkits die in de handel beschikbaar zijn. Overtuig er u van dat welke kit u ook koopt, hij metingen doet naar carbonaat- en bicarbonaat-hardheid(dKH) en niet naar kalk- of magnesiumhardheid (dH).

Is de dKH te laag, dan kan u leidingwater toevoegen (hoge carbonaat-hardheid). Indien de dKH nog hoger moet dan kan u natrium-bicarbonaat gebruiken maar dit is meestal niet nodig tenzij u in uw aquarium gedestilleerd of gezuiverd water gebruikt.

Meestal is de dKH-waarde eerder te hoog dan te laag. Is die te hoog, voeg dan gedestilleerd water toe of water dat werd gezuiverd via deïonisatie en omkeerosmose. Deze twee zuiveringsmetoden worden beschreven in de volgende paragraaf. Weet echter dat niet alle metoden om zacht water te maken meteen ook de dKH reduceren.

dH heeft betrekking op waterhardheid: de concentratie aan kalkionen (Ca+) en magnesiumionen (Mg+). Wanneer de concentratie van deze ionen te hoog is noemen wij het water "hard." Een kleine concentratie van deze ionen betekent "zacht" water.

*Waterscheikunde — "zacht" water maken:* In de meeste gevallen is het water dat hobbyisten ter beschikking hebben hard, zodat de vraag naar "hard" water niet zo vaak voorkomt. Mocht u dan toch hard water nodig hebben, dan zijn er in de handel producten beschikbaar die het verharden van water op een snelle en eenvoudige manier mogelijk maken. Voor de meeste aquarianen is het wel een probleem om "zacht" water te maken, water met een lage dKH-en dH-waarde.

*Regenwater:* Omdat regenwater geen Ca+, Mg+ noch bicarbonaten bevat is het dikwijls een ideale bron voor zacht water. Alhoewel, in geïndustrialiseerde gebieden zijn hoge concentraties polluerende stoffen zoals zwaveldioxide en waterstofchloride aanwezig, die onvermijdelijk in het regenwater terecht komen.

Wanneer u woont in een niet vervuilde omgeving kan regenwater een goede gok betekenen. Nochtans zal het toch nodig zijn om er een hoeveelheid chloorvrij kraantjeswater aan toe te voegen om de gepaste dKH- en dH-waarde te bekomen.

*Gedestilleerd water:* Dit soort water is de meest voorkomende vorm van zuiver water. Een beetje te zuiver echter! Omdat het in wezen geen mineralen meer bevat met nog slechts enkele opgeloste gassen, verbreekt gedestilleerd water de osmosebalans, de wisselwerking, tussen water en levende organismen.

De balans is verstoord omdat mineralen en andere substanties door osmose van uit het organisme van de plant in het water worden gezogen: deze mineralen en substanties neigen naar een gelijke concentratie aan beide zijden van het half-doorlaatcodee membraan van de plant. Deze "gelijkschakeling" kan de planten doden. Wanneer u dus beslist om gedestilleerd water te gebruiken, vermeng het dan met kraantjeswater om de vereiste dKH te bekomen. Maar, voor een groot aquarium is gedestilleerd water vrij duur en het is geen goede prijs/kwaliteit oplossing.

*Omkeerosmose:* Een omkeerosmose apparaat produceert zacht water, (gelijkaardig aan gedestilleerd water), door gebruik te maken van druk om ionen te dwingen te diffunderen doorheen een half-doorlatend membraan. Onthou dat water, gezuiverd met een osmoseeenheid nooit zo zuiver zal zijn als gedestilleerd water. Toestellen die voor hobbyisten beschikbaar zijn kunnen immers nooit genoeg druk leveren voor het bekomen van werkelijk zuiver water. Ze kunnen echter wel voldoende calciumionen (Ca+), Magnesiumionen (Mg+) en bicarbonaten uit het water verwijderen om het te kunnen gebruiken in een aangeplant aquarium.

# Inleiding Tot Aquariumplanten

**Veenmos:** Veen-of turfmos maakt het water zacht door zich te verbinden met Ca+ en Mg+ terwijl het taninnezuur en galzuur vrijgeeft. Dit verhoogt de zuurheid van het water, waardoor sommige bicarbonaten omgevormd worden tot $CO_2$ dat op zijn beurt het dKH-gehalte naar beneden haalt. Al is veenmos voor het verzachten van water, gezien de prijs/kwaliteit, een der beste metoden, het heeft toch enkele nadelen. Het werkt trager dan de meeste andere metoden en vaak niet zo grondig. Het verlaagt de dKH onvoldoende en geeft het water een geelachtige kleur.

Die gele kleur kan worden weggenomen door hoogwaardige kool in een mechanisch filter te gebruiken. Maar, kool verhoogt het pH en dKH-gehalte door carbonaten in het water vrij te laten. Hoeveel daarvan wordt vrijgegeven hangt af van het asgehalte van de kool.

Waterverzachting met behulp van harsen: Harsen worden op twee manieren gebruikt om water te verzachten: de natrium-verzachting en de deïonisatie. Van deze beide is de laatste veruit de beste. De natrium-verzachting is in wezen onbruikbaar als verzachter voor water dat is bestemd voor planten. Bij deze metode worden immers (Ca+ en Mg+) kationen gewoon vervangen door (Na+) kationen. Nochthans denken velen verkeerdelijk dat water geschikt is voor een beplant aquarium wanneer het geen calcium of magnesium ionen bevat.

*Natriumontharding:* Bij deze methode wordt een materie, "kationisch hars in natriumvorm" genaamd, commerciëel gebruikt om water te verzachten. Doch, chemisch gesproken verwijdert deze substantie niet alle kationen (zoals die van natrium) die bijdragen tot de hardheid. Bovendien worden geen carbonaten en bicarbonaten verwijderd. Met andere woorden, de dKH-waarde wordt niet verlaagd.

*Deïonisatiemethode:* Deze metode om water zacht te maken is beter dan de voorgaande. Bij deïonisatie worden twee harsen gebruikt: een kationisch hars met waterstofgedrag (bestaat uit positief geladen ionen) en een anionisch hars met waterstofgedrag (negatieve ionen).

Het kationische hars vervangt de positief geladen ionen in het water (waaronder Na+ en Mg+) door waterstofionen (H+). Terzelfdertijd voorziet het anionische hars het chloride, de bicarbonaten en de carbonaten van een negatief geladen molecule OH–. Een neveneffect van dit proces is, dat de resulterende vrije waterstof H+ en OH– samen water vormen ($H_2O$).

Water dat op die manier werd gezuiverd elimineert zowel de Ca+ en Mg+ hardheid als de carbonaathardheid (dKH). Het resulterende water is gelijkwaardig aan gedestilleerd water. Zoals voor gedestilleerd water is het aanbevelenswaardig om kraantjeswater toe te voegen om de juiste dKH-waarde te bekomen.

Wanneer de harsen verzadigd zijn met chloride en carbonaat moet elk van hen "herladen" worden met een sterk zuur of vervangen door nieuw hars. Ik geef u de goede raad dat herladen van het hars niet zelf te doen. Zuren zijn extreem gevaarlijk.

**pH, dKH, dH en CO2:** de carbonaathardheid (dKH), zuurheid en hoeveelheid kooldioxide bepalen samen de kwaliteit van het water. Het ene beïnvloedt het andere. De pH van uw aquarium wordt bepaald door het niveau $CO_2$ en de dKH. $CO_2$ wekt koolzuur op dat de pH van het water verlaagt. De dKH (carbonaat hardheid) werkt als een buffer die de pH stabiliseert. Wanneer de dKH het ideale niveau van 3 graden bereikt, belet het de pH te dalen onder de 6.7 wanneer CO2 wordt toegevoerd. Is de dKH te laag dan zal een

kleine hoeveelheid $CO_2$ de pH waarde ver onder de 6.7 brengen tot een gevaarlijke waarde. Is de dKH te hoog dan zullen zelfs hoge hoeveelheden $CO_2$ het alkalisch gedrag (hoge pH) niet beïnvloeden.

De dKH-waarde kan dus indirect worden bepaald door het meten van de pH. Indien $CO_2$ wordt geinjecteerd dan moet de pH evenredig dalen. Indien die pH-waarde daalt, maar niet onder de 6.7 komt, dan is de dKH-waarde ideaal. Komt de pH-waarde onder de 6.7 dan is de dKH te laag. Omgekeerd, wanneer toevoegen van $CO_2$ de pH niet evenredig doet dalen tot 6.7 – 7.2, dan is de dKH te hoog.

Tenslotte, indien u de geschikte dKH-waarde (ongeveer 3 graden) aanhoudt, dan zal de dH automatisch binnen aanneembare grenzen voor "zacht water" gelegen zijn. Dit is trouwens de reden waarom ik niet veel tijd heb gespendeerd aan de dH. Alle metoden die daarnet werden behandeld om water zacht te maken (door dKH controle) zullen de dH verlagen. Zij reduceren allemaal de hoeveelheid bicarbonaten in het water (dKH) evenals de concentratie aan Ca+ en Mg+ (dH). De enige uitzondering is de natrium verzachting die dan ook niet wordt aanbevolen.

**Omgevingsfactoren en waterkwaliteit:** Veel decoratieve elementen die u in uw aquarium wenst te plaatsen (kienhout, rotsen, kiezel) kunnen de kwaliteit en de scheikundige samenstelling van uw aquariumwater veranderen. Voorbeeld: sommige rotsen en kiezel kunnen calcium aan het water afgeven en kienhout bevat verscheidene chemische bestanddelen die in het aquarium terechtkomen. Voor kienhout raad ik aan het te koken of uitgebreid te drenken en verder, rotsen en kiezel te kiezen die vrij zijn van calcium of mineralen die de carbonaathardheid (dKH) van het water kunnen verhogen.

## Algen — En Slakkencontrole

**Algencontrole:** Al wie ooit een aquarium heeft gehad is vertrouwd met de frustratie die algengroei kan bezorgen. Het is niet alleen onaantrekkelijk maar algen belemmeren bovendien de ademhaling en de fotosynthese wanneer zij de bladeren van de planten overgroeien. Wees speciaal op uw hoede voor de gladde donkergroene gelatineachtige film die blauwe alg (cyanobacteriën) wordt genoemd. In aanwezigheid van hoge nitraat, en fosfaat-concentraties groeit blauwe alg uitermate snel en kan zeer vlug de planten verstikken. Van alle algen schijnt dit type het moeilijkst te zijn om uit te roeien gezien er ook geen enkele vis is, die het zal eten. Nochthans is er, voor zover ik weet, geen product dat blauwe alg kan vernietigen. Voorkomen is echter nog altijd beter dan genezen: hou nitraat- en fosfaat concentraties in uw aquarium binnen de normale grenzen.

Onbeheerste algengroei schijnt een typich probleem te zijn bij een nieuw-opgezet aquarium. Hierna volgen enkele suggesties die zullen helpen bij de algencontrole in uw aquarium.

(1) Voorzie algen-etende vissen zoals de Octocinclus, Epalzeorhynchus siamensis, dwerg Plecostomus en de meeste levendcodeenden van de Poeciliidae familie. Noteer wel dat de familie der Plecostomus snelgroeiende vissen zijn waarvan sommigen ook planten eten: geen goede keuze dus. De corydoras soorten horen ook in uw aquarium thuis om het grind te beroeren en te beletten dat algen zich op de bodem zouden vastzetten. Van zodra uw beplant aquarium klaar is kan u er algen-etende vissen inbrengen: laat niet toe dat er een

algenprobleem ontstaat voor dat u algen-etende vissen hebt uitgezet. De meeste vissen zullen niet in staat zijn om voldoende algen te eten in een reeds overgroeid aquarium. Voedt de vissen daarom spaarzaam zodat ze zich verplicht voelen om algen te eten.

(2) Beplant uw aquarium voldoende van bij het begin. Voeg er ook veel snelgroeiende planten aan toe: veel van de zogeheten "stekplanten" (planten die zijn gegroeid uit stekken en verkocht in bosjes) vallen hieronder. Snelgroeiende planten onderdrukken de algengroei.

(3) Ververs om de week (hoogstens om de ander week) de helft van het aquariumwater om het stikstofhoudende afval en de fosfaten die de algengroei bevorderen, te verwijderen.

(4) Indien al deze middelen falen, dan raden sommigen aan het water te hehandelen met een zwakke koperoplossing die de koperconcentratie het aquarium brengt tot een niveau van 0.3...0.5 ppm. Dat is echter de oplossing van de laatste kans!

Koperoplossingen kunnen algen doden maar ook de planten en de vissen. Deze methode is erg betwistbaar en ik raad ze derhalve niet aan – alhoewel veel commerciële plantenkwekers koperoplossingen gebruiken. Wanneer u toch beslist om deze methode te gebruiken let dan op enkele zaken: zelfs bij het gebruik van een minieme dosis koper kan een klein percentage planten afsterven. Deze "kopergevoelige" planten worden vermeld bij de informatiecode van elke soort. Verdere gegevens hierover kan u vinden in de gids voor de gebruiker van dit boek.

Doe preciese metingen wanneer u koper gebruikt: het leven van uw planten en vissen hangt evan af. In elk geval, eens gedaan, wees dan zeker van de hoeveelheid koper in het water of gebruik een actief koolfilter om het koper te verwijderen.

Slakkencontrole: De meeste slakken kunnen verwoestend werk aanrichten in een beplant aquarium. Soorten als de Ampullaria paludosa en de soorten Marisa Rotula, hebben een vraatzuchtige honger naar planten. De Ampullaria cuprina die veel worden gebruikt bij de bestrijding van algen, eten ook planten. Een eenvoudige methode om het slakkenbestand in bedwang te houden is enkele slakkenetende vissen in het aquarium te plaatsen: onder hen de Tetra odon. Het nadeel van dergelijke vissen is dat ze agressief zijn. Ze bijten naar de andere vissen en zullen de kleinere als voedsel aanzien indien ze die kunnen vangen. Botia macracantha en andere kleine Botia soorten zijn een betere keuze. Een 6 cm grote Botia kan gemakkelijk kleine slakken elemineren in een tijd van enkele dagen.

# Comparing Methods

There is a vast difference between the quality of plants raised in an outdoor environment with no special care vs. in an indoor aquarium setup according to the methods described in this book (in the section *Introduction to Aquarium Plants*). This section was designed to highlight that difference in the most dramatic way I know how.

The photos on the following pages speak for themselves. Each frame show two photos of the same plant — the main picture displays a plant grown in a properly setup aquarium; the smaller photo inset within the main frame shows the plant as it appeared after 120 days outside. As you will see, the plants grown under the "hands-off" natural conditions are quite pathetic compared to those carefully cultivated in the aquarium. Also, a significant portion of the plants grown outside simply died.

Each example is labeled; this label indicates how many days the healthy plant (shown in the main photo frame) was cared for under the ideal growing conditions in an aquarium.

All of the "before" examples were kept for 120 days outside. The conditions, both before and after, under which the plants were kept are listed below. Note that the pots found in both the "before" and the "after" photos are the same size. This was done to provide a reference point for your comparisons.

## Outdoor Conditions:

- Outdoors for 120 days.
- Extremely high dH and dKH water ( from South Florida, whose ground is coral-based and therefore high in carbonate hardness and calcium).
- pH above pH8.0
- Kept under Nursery Shade, allowing approximately 80% sunlight to enter.
- 300 gallon tanks with continuous running water.
- Each tank contained approximately 100 1.5" swordtail fish.
- Daily feedings of the fish were performed.

## Aquarium Conditions:

- *Note: the conditions provided below are those that are specific to this setup. The remaining factors are described in the "Introduction to Aquarium Plants" section of this book.*
- 100 gallon, 20 in. high tank with 3.5 watts light-per-gallon (350 watts) — full-spectrum VHO flourescent lighting.
- Rainwater mixed with a small amount of well-water.

After 45 Days/Ideal Growing Conditions

After 45 Days/Ideal Growing Conditions

*After 45 Days/Ideal Growing Conditions*

*After 60 Days/Ideal Growing Conditions*

*After 45 Days/Ideal Growing Conditions*

▼ *After 90 Days/Ideal Growing Conditions*

▼ *After 90 Days/Ideal Growing Conditions*

# Aquascaping

# Aquascaping

Learning how to maintain healthy plants is of the utmost importance when creating a spectacular aquascape. No matter how artistic a person is, if the plants are not thriving, then creating a beautiful planted aquarium is virtually impossible. Yet, if the plants in your aquarium are healthy, even a poorly designed aquascape can be visually pleasing.

The suggestions here are by no means the only way to create a beautiful aquarium. After all, beauty is in the eye of the beholer. All artistic pursuits should be based upon individual taste and creativity; there is no right or wrong way of designing an aquarium.

Bear in mind that if your design is not up to your expectations it is not a tragedy. You can always rearrange it. My personal philosophy on designing an aquascape is based on capturing the brilliant colors of Van Gogh, while still making it look natural.

## Overall Shape (The Environment):

**A Side-slope Style:** As seen in the photograph (in the fold-out section), one side of the aquarium starts with an open space (like a meadow). Gradually, the plants increase in height as you move across the aquarium.

**B Mount (Mountain) Style:** In this style, both sides of the aquarium have low plants. As you move toward the center, the plants gradually increase in height. This forms the shape of a mountain. In my opinion, this "mountain" will look more natural (and, therefore, pleasing) if it is placed off-center within your aquarium.

**C Valley Style:** This is essentially the inverse of the Mount Style; both sides of the aquarium are planted with tall plants that gradually decrease in height toward the center of the tank. This creates a valley. As a rule, I suggest that the height, size, and grade of the two slopes should not be uniform with one another. Also—like the Mount Style—the "valley" should not be perfectly centered in your aquarium.

**D Front-slope Style:** In this arrangement, the tallest plants are placed in the rear of the aquarium, and the height of the plants decrease as they approach the front. Keep in mind that the front section needs short plants. This creates open space in the front of your tank.

## Plant Shape

The shape and form of the plant leaves should be taken into consideration in order to emphasize the distinct charactersitics of the various plants in your aquarium. For example, if you plant a fine-feathered leaf plant in front, try to used broader-leaf plants in the rear. Such varied arrangements will make each group of plants distinct from one another and make your tank more visually interesting.

## Color

As with the shape of the plants, I believe the color of the plants in your aquarium should be varied. Personally, I do not like a uniformly green aquarium, because the plants tend to blend into each other. A more striking visual effect may be achieved by either coordinating different colors or using contrasting shades of green. For example, if a light green plant is in front, use another color (or darker green plant) behind it—or vice versa. In nature, a field of wildflowers has randomly contrasting colors, and yet the whole has a unified, coherent "look" that in universally considered beautiful.

## Height, Space and Grouping

Shorter plants should be in front. The height of your plants should increase toward the back of the aquarium. Combining an open space (usually in front), and a densely planted area increases the depth of field within your aquarium, making the tank seem larger. Plants of the same species should be planted in close proximity with one another, rather than being scattered throughout the aquarium. In nature, plants of the same species tend to grow together.

## Texture

The combination of driftwood, rocks and living plants creates a diversity of textures that simulates the look of a natural aquascape. Another benefit of this approach is that it breaks up a monotonous environment.

Finally, I do not believe in providing diagrams of where certain species should be planted in certain areas. You should treat your aquarium as a canvas. What you decide to paint is entirely up to your inviduality and creativity!

# Landschaftsgestaltung Im Wasser

Wenn man eine spektakuläre Landschaftsgestaltung im Wasser schafft, ist es äußerst wichtig, zu lernen, wie man sich gesunde Pflanzen hält. Egal, wie künstlerisch begabt eine Person ist, wenn die Pflanzen nicht gedeihen, ist es praktisch unmöglich, ein wunderschönes bepflanztes Aquarium zu schaffen. Wenn die Pflanzen in Ihrem Aquarium jedoch gesund sind, kann selbst eine schlecht angelegte Landschaftsgestaltung optisch erfreulich sein.

Die hier abgegebenen Vorschläge sind keinesfalls die einzige Art und Weise, auf die ein wunderschönes Aquarium geschaffen werden kann. Jedem gefällt ja schließlich etwas anderes. Alle künstlerischen Unternehmungen sollten auf Kreativität und individuellem Geschmack beruhen; es gibt keine richtige oder falsche Art für das Design eines Aquariums.

Denken Sie daran, daß es keine Tragödie ist, wenn Ihr Design Ihren Erwartungen nicht entspricht. Sie können es immer noch neu anordnen.

Meine persönliche Philosophie über den Entwurf einer Landschaftsgestaltung im Wasser basiert darauf, die lebhaften Farben von Van Gogh einzufangen, während sie gleichzeitig natürlich aussieht.

## Stile

**Ⓐ Seitlich abfallend:** Wie auf dem Foto zu sehen ist, hat eine Seite des Aquariums ein offenes Gelände (wie eine Wiese). Die Pflanzen werden zur anderen Seite des Aquariums hin allmählich höher.

**Ⓑ Berg:** Bei diesem Stil befinden sich auf beiden Seiten des Aquariums niedrige Pflanzen. Zur Mitte hin werden die Pflanzen allmählich höher, und bilden einen Berg. Meiner Meinung nach sieht dieser „Berg" natürlicher (und daher nett) aus, wenn er sich nicht exakt in der Mitte des Aquariums befindet.

**Ⓒ Tal:** Dies ist praktisch das Gegenteil zum Berg; beide Seiten des Aquariums sind mit hohen Pflanzen bepflanzt, die zur Mitte hin allmählich niedriger werden. Hierdurch wird ein Tal geschaffen. Generell würde ich vorschlagen, daß Höhe, Form und Gefälle der beiden Abhänge nicht identisch sein sollte. Außerdem sollte sich das „Tal"—genau wie beim Berg —nicht exakt in der Mitte des Aquariums befinden.

**Ⓓ Nach vorne abfallend:** Bei diesem Stil werden die höchsten Pflanzen hinten im Aquarium angepflanzt und die Pflanzen werden zur Vorderseite des Aquariums hin kleiner. Denken Sie daran, daß vorne kurze Pflanzen benötigt werden. Hierdurch wird auf der Vorderseite des Aquariums ein offenes Gelände geschaffen.

## Farbe

Mir persönlich gefällt ein einheitlich grünes Aquarium nicht, weil die Pflanzen ineinander übergehen. Wenn entweder verschiedene Farben miteinander koordiniert oder kontrastierende Grüntöne verwendet werden, kann ein eindrucksvollerer optischer Effekt erzielt werden. Wenn sich z.B. im Vordergrund eine hellgrüne Pflanze befindet, verwenden Sie hinter ihr eine andere Farbe (oder eine Pflanze mit einem dunkleren Grün) — oder umgekehrt. In der Natur hat ein Feld mit Wildblumen zufällig kontrastierende Farben und trotzdem hat es insgesamt ein zusammenhängendes „Erscheinungsbild", das universell als wunderschön angesehen wird.

## Form

Die Gestalt und Form der Pflanzenblätter sollte ebenfalls in Erwägung gezogen werden, um die individuellen Besonderheiten der verschiedenen Pflanzen im Aquarium hervorzuheben. Wenn Sie z.B. im Vordergrund eine Pflanze mit fein gefederten Blättern pflanzen, verwenden Sie im Hintergrund Pflanzen mit breiteren Blättern. Solche variierten Arrangements heben jede Gruppe Pflanzen von anderen Gruppen ab, und machen Ihr Aquarium optisch interessanter.

## Höhe und Offene Gelände

Niedrigere Pflanzen sollten sich vorne befinden. Die Pflanzen sollte zur Rückwand des Aquariums hin höher werden.

Wenn ein offenes Gelände (normalerweise im Vordergrund) mit einem dicht bepflanzten Bereich kombiniert wird, erhöht sich die Feldtiefe im Aquarium und es sieht größer aus.

## Struktur

Die Kombination von Treibholz, Steinen und lebenden Pflanzen erzeugt eine Vielfalt an Strukturen, die das „Erscheinungsbild" einer natürlichen Landschaft unter Wasser simulieren. Ein weiterer Vorteil ist, daß eine monotone Umgebung aufgelockert wird.

## Gruppierung

Pflanzen der selben Spezies sollten nahe zusammen gepflanzt werden, anstatt sie im Aquarium zu verteilen. In der Natur neigen Pflanzen der selben Spezies dazu, nebeneinander zu wachsen.

Letztendlich halte ich nichts davon, Diagramme abzubilden, die zeigen, wo bestimmte Spezies in bestimmten Bereichen angepflanzt werden sollten. Sie sollten Ihr Aquarium wie eine Leinwand behandeln. Es ist ganz und gar Ihrer Individualität und Kreativität überlassen, was Sie malen wollen.

# Paysages aquatiques

Il est de la plus grande importance d'apprendre à entretenir des plantes en bonne santé pour obtenir un paysage aquatique à la beauté spectaculaire. Le sens artistique de chacun n'entre pas en ligne de compte lorsque les plantes ne sont pas bien tenues. En effet, l'aquarium mal entretenu ne pourra pas jamais être beau. En revanche, si les plantes de votre aquarium sont en bonne santé, le paysage le plus sobre pourra être visuellement plaisant. Les suggestions données ci-dessous ne sont pas l'unique façon de construire un bel aquarium. Après tout, le concept de beauté est très subjectif. Toute création artistique devrait être basée sur le goût individuel et la créativité de chacun. Le design d'un aquarium ne peut être bon ou mauvais.

Ne vous inquiétez pas si vous ne parvenez pas à réaliser le paysage que vous aviez imaginé. Il vous suffira de réaménager l'aquarium selon vos souhaits. Ma philosophie personnelle dans ce domaine est basée sur la capacité de capter les couleurs à la façon de Van Gogh, to ut en conservant un style naturel.

## Différents Styles

**Ⓐ Formation de pente latérale:** Comme illustré par la photo, une partie de l'aquarium commence par un espace ouvert ( comme une prairie). Progressivement, la taille des plantes augmente jusqu'à l'autre bout de l'aquarium.

**Ⓑ Formation montagneuse:** Des plantes basses sont placées des deux côtés de l'aquarium. En déplaçant le regard vers le centre de l'aquarium, la taille des plantes augmente pour donner l'aspect d'une montagne. A mon sens, cette "montagne"donnera une impression plus naturelle (et plus belle) si le sommet de la "montagne" est légèrement excentré.

**Ⓒ Formation d'une vallée:** Ce design est à l'opposé du style montagneux. Les deux côtés de l'aquarium sont plantés avec des plantes hautes dont la taille décroît en allant vers le centre. L'impression d'une vallée est donnée. Je conseillerais de ne pas placer les plantes de façon symétrique pour éviter toute uniformité. Comme pour la formation montagneuse, je conseille d'excentrer le centre de la vallée.

**Ⓓ Formation d'une pente vers l'avant:** Pour ce modèle, les plantes les plus grandes sont plantées à l'arrière de l'aquarium, et la hauteur des plantes décroît jusqu'à l'avant de l'aquarium. Prenez garde de bien placer des plantes restant petites à l'avant de l'aquarium. Vous créerez ainsi un espace ouvert à l'avant de l'aquarium.

## Couleurs

Personnellement, je n'apprécie pas un aquarium du même vert, sans aucunes nuances de couleurs, car alors les plantes ne sont pas mises en valeur. Un effet visuel peut être réussi en coordonnant différentes colorations ou en utilisant des variations de "tons" de vert. Par exemple, si une plante vert-clair est placée à l'avant, placez une plante plus foncée en arrière-plan pour les mettre en valeur, ou vice-versa. Dans la nature, un champs de fleurs sauvages a des couleurs très contrastées, bien que l'aspect général reste cohérent, et soit admiré par tous.

## Forme des plantes/Hauteur/Espace

La forme et l'aspect des feuilles des plantes devrait être pris en considération afin d'accentuer les caractéristiques distinctes des diverses variétés de plantes aquatiques. Par exemple, si vous placez une plante aux feuilles fines et duveteuses en avant-plan, essayez de placer des plantes aux feuilles plus larges en arrière-plan.

La diversité de tels arrangements mettra en valeur chaque groupe de plantes et rendra votre aquarium plus attractif. Les plantes les plus basses peuvent être placées en avant-plan de l'aquarium. La taille de vos plantes grandira plus vous déplacerez votre regard vers le fond de l'aquarium. Lorsque l'on sait combiner des espaces ouverts (normalement en avant-plan de l'aquarium) avec des espaces plantés densément, on parvient à augmenter la profondeur du champs visuel et vous donnez l'impression que l'aquarium est plus large.

## Texture

La combinaison de racines, de pierres et de plantes vivantes provoque une grande diversité de textures qui simule le "look" d'un paysage aquatique naturel. Un autre avantage réside dans le fait qu'un tel procédé brise la monotonie du paysage.

## Ensemble

Les plantes de la même variété devraient être plantées à proximité dans le même ensemble plutôt que d'être disséminées dans tout l'aquarium. Dans la nature les plantes d'une même espèce tendent à se développer au même endroit. Pour conclure, je ne crois pas à ces diagrammes qui vous indiquent à quel endroit planter vos plantes. Il vous faut traiter votre aquarium comme un tableau. Ce que vous désirez peindre dépend entièrement de votre individualité et de votre créativité.

# Onderwaterlandschappen

Bij het ontwerp van een spectaculair onderwaterlandschap is het uitermate belangrijk te weten hoe u planten in goede gezondheid kan houden. Bij zo'n ontwerp leidt gevoel voor kunst tot niets indien de planten slecht gedijen: zo'n aquarium, amper onderhouden, is hoedanook nooit mooi. Daarentegen zal het uitzicht van uw aquarium u veel kijkgenot bezorgen wanneer de planten gezond zijn, ook al is de aanplanting eerder sober. De raadgevingen die wij u geven zijn niet de enige manier om een mooi aquarium uit te bouwen want schoonheid is een subjectief gegeven. Het zoeken naar die schoonheid hangt af van persoonlijke smaak en creativiteit zodat de vraag, goed of niet goed, bij het ontwerp van een aquarium eigenlijk niet hoeft gesteld te worden. En, het is echt geen tragedie wanneer het resultaat niet beantwoordt aan uw verwachtingen: herbeginnen kan altijd.

Ik blijf ervan overtuigd dat, wanneer het gaat om het ontwerp van een aquarium, het mogelijk moet zijn om de briljante kleuren van Van Gogh te introduceren in het natuurlijk kader van een onderwaterlandschap.

## Algemene opbouw

**A Hellend vlak:** Zoals dat in bijgaande foto wordt geillustreerd wordt aan één zijde een open ruimte gecreëerd - zoals een soort weide. Tot aan de andere kant van het aquarium neemt de hoogte der planten geleidelijk toe.

**B Bergland:** Aan beide zijden van het aquarium worden kleine planten geplaatst. Naar het midden toe worden die groter. Volgens mij zal deze "berg" heel wat natuurlijker (en derhalve mooier) lijken wanneer hij niet pal in het midden van het aquarium wordt geplaatst.

**C Valei:** Dit ontwerp is het tegendeel van het voorgaande: beide zijden van het aquarium zijn begroeid met hoge planten die geleidelijk naar het centrum toe in hoogte afnemen waardoor de indruk van een dal wordt gewekt. Een goede raad: maak de beide hellingen verschillend om diversiteit in het landschap te verkrijgen. Evenzo - zoals dat bij een berglandschap het geval was - maken we het dal niet in het midden van het aquarium.

**D Frontale helling:** Voor dit model worden de grootste planten achteraan in het aquarium geplaatst waarbij de hoogte der begroeiing afneemt naar de voorzijde toe. Vooraan komen dus kleine plantjes waardoor daar een open ruimte ontstaat.

## Kleur

Persoonlijk hou ik niet van een uniform-groen aquarium omdat hierdoor de planten afzonderlijk niet tot hun recht komen. Een levendiger beeld krijgt men door verschillende kleuren of diverse tinten van groen te gebruiken. Een voorbeeld: achter een lichtgroene plant op de voorgrond plaatst u liefst een donkergroene of een anders gekleurde. Vergelijken we even met de vrije natuur waar een veld met wilde bloemen bestaat uit exemplaren met sterk contrasterende kleuren. Toch vormen zij een harmonisch geheel, een harmonie die wij "mooi" noemen.

## Het uiterlijk der planten

We moeten rekening houden met het model en de vorm der bladeren om de verschillende karakteristieken der waterplanten te kunnen benadrukken. Fijne, donzige blaadjes op de voorgrond vragen om een achtergrond van brede bladeren. Door op die manier variatie te brengen in de aanplant komt elke plantengroep los te staan van de andere waardoor uw aquarium aantrekkelijker wordt.

## Hoogte/RuimteOpbouw

Kleine planten horen thuis op de voorgrond. Hoe groter de plant hoe verder zij naar de achtergrond moet geplaatst worden.

Door open ruimten (liefst op de voorgrond) te combineren met dicht aangeplante zones, vergroot u het dieptezicht van uw aquarium waardoor die groter gaat lijken.

## Opbouw

De combinatie van kienhout, rotsen en levende planten veroorzaakt een grote variatie in het aquarium-patroon waardoor het uitzicht van een natuurlijke onderwaterwereld wordt benaderd.

## Groeperen

Planten van dezelfde variëteit worden best in elkaars nabijheid geplaatst, liever dan ze te verspreiden over het hele aquarium. In de natuur groeien planten van éénzelfde soort ook het liefst in elkaars omgeving.

Tot besluit nog dit: ik geloof niet in de gegevens uit grafieken die vertellen waar de beste plaats is voor die of die variëteit. Beschouw uw aquarium als een onbeschilderd doek: wat u wil schilderen, hangt volledig af van uw persoonlijkheid en creativiteit!

# User's Guide

## Organization of the Book.

*Aquarium Plants: The Practical Guide* is divided into three basic sections: True Aquarium Plants, Terrestrial Plants, and Floating Plants. Almost all of the book is dedicated to the *True Aquarium Plants* section. Most pages in this section describe two plant   A variety of information is provided for each plant in an at-a-glance format that we call an "Information Bar," which is described in the *Information Bar* section of this User's Guide.

*Floating Plants* is a smaller section that lists the most commonly seen true aquatic plants that float on the surface. Although they are true aquatic plants that thrive in water, they are not good aquarium plants because they block light from reaching the submerged aquarium plants. The floating are basically pond plants, and this section is included only to show plants that are *not recommended* for home aquariums.

Finally, a third section—*Terrestrial Plants*—lists plants that are not aquatic yet are sometimes used in aquariums. This section's purpose is basically to show you what plants *not* to use in your aquarium. They will die. Therefore, only a small photo and the name is given for each variety in this section. *All the inform-ation in remaining sections of this User's Guide only applies to the True Aquarium Plants section of the book.*

## Organization of the page.

Most pages in the *True Aquarium Plant* section have two to three plants. A label, such as Ⓐ will appear next to both the photo of a plant and its appropriate Information.

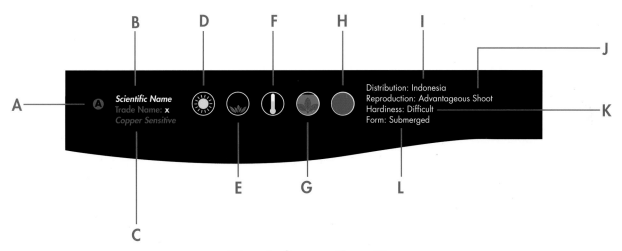

## The Information Bar.

The Information Bar provides facts about the plants in a simple, at-a-glance format. Below is an example of the Information Bar. The icons and text always appear in the same order.

**A. The Identification Label:** The number label on the far left of the bar corresponds to a number next to one of the plant photos on the page. This number links the photo and information about that plant.

**B. The Name Line:** The name lines located on the left of the Information Bar can contain up to three lines. The following items may be included: (1) the scientific name of the plant (genus and species), (2) a common trade name for that plant, and (3) the *copper sensitive* (explained below), may also appear.

**C. The Copper Sensitive Line:** This orange line —located under the name lines — does not appear in every entry. It is only displayed when a plant cannot tolerate *any* quantity of copper or copper sulfate in the water.

# User's Guide

**D. Light Requirements Icon:** Different plants thrive under different lighting conditions. This icon informs you of each plant's *minimum* lighting requirements. The icons and their meanings are shown below. The watts given for the lighting requirements are for tanks 50 cm (20") deep or less. Also, the watts given for each icon are *watts-per-3.78 liters* (*1 gallon*) with full-spectrum flourescent tubes.

*Bright: 3.5– 4.5 watts*     *Medium: 2.5– 3.0 watts*     *Low: 1.5– 2.0 watts*

**E. Plant Positioning Icon:** The purpose of this icon is fairly self explanatory. Plants can be classified as foreground, midground, or background, based on their height and structure. For example: a thin, tall plant would be classified as *background*, while a low, ground-hugging plant would be a *foreground* plant.

*Foreground*     *Midground*     *Background*

**F. Temperature Icon:** This icon (a thermometer, of course) indicates the ideal range of temperatures in which a plant will thrive. It is fairly important that you keep your aquarium's water within the range that is optimal for that plant , no matter what the environment outside the tank is. Most plants tend to fall in the medium temperature range. The various temperature icons and their  meanings are shown below.

*High: 84–86° F.*     *Medium: 73–83° F.*     *Low: 64–72° F.*
*(29–30° C.)*          *(23–28° C.)*           *(18–22° C.)*

**G. Environment Icon:** This icon tells whether a true aquarium plant is *amphibious* (meaning that it can thrive either totally or partially submerged) or whether it is a *submerged* plant, capable only of existing totally underwater.

*Submerged*     *Amphibious*

**H. pH Icon:** This icon indicates the optimal pH range for growing each plant species in your tank. Each colored disk represents a different pH range. The icons and their meanings are shown below.

*Alkaline: pH 7.1–8.0*     *Neutral: pH 7.0*     *Acid: pH 6.9–6.0*

# User's Guide

**I. Distribution Information Line:** This line (marked by the word *distribution*) informs you where the plant is generally found in nature.

**J. Reproduction Method Information Line:** Plants reproduce in a variety of ways. This line (marked by the word *reproduction* ) tells you the method of reproduction for each variety:

> **Rhizome:** Plants that produce shoots stemming from a thick rootlike stem. The rhizomes can be cut away from the main plant and planted individually.

> **Bulb:** Plants grown from a bulbous base that sends roots down and leaves upward.

> **Cutting:** Plants that develop roots from nodes at the stem of the main plant. These can be separated into a new plant.

> **Advantageous Shoot:** The mother plant produces flowering shoots that form new plants ; also, new plants can form from old leaves.

> **Runners:** Horizontal, creeping stems that extend from a plant and that possess stolens (small nut-like bulbs) from which new plants develop.

> **Seeds & Spores:** This method is not commonly used by hobbyists because the plants generally take a long time to develop to full size.

**K. Hardiness Information Line:** This line (indicated by the word hardiness ) tells you whether it is easy, moderate, or difficult to maintain a particular plant in an aquarium. You may want to note that all plants in the *Terrarium Plants* section are essentially doomed in an aquarium.

**L. Form Information Line:** This line (marked by the word *form*) tells you whether the plant in the photo shown was grown in *submerged* grown completely underwater, or *emerged (emerged)* grown out of the water.

# Hinweise Für Den Benutzer

## Aufgliederung dieses Buchs

Aquariumpflanzen: Ein praktischer Leitfaden ist in drei grundlegende Abschnitte unterteilt: Echte Aquariumpflanzen, Erdpflanzen und Schwimmende Pflanzen. Fast das gesamte Buch ist dem Abschnitt *Echte Aquariumpflanzen* gewidmet. Auf den meisten Seiten in diesem Abschnitt werden zwei Pflanzen beschrieben. Für jede Pflanze wird in einem Format, das wir den „Informationsbalken" nennen, auf einen Blick eine Vielfalt an Informationen geboten. Dieser Balken wird im Abschnitt Informationsbalken dieser Hinweise für den Benutzer beschrieben.

Schwimmende Pflanzen ist ein kleinerer Abschnitt, in dem die echten Wasserpflanzen beschrieben werden, die man am öftesten an der Oberfläche schwimmen sieht. Obwohl es sich hier um echte Wasserpflanzen handelt, die im Wasser gedeihen, sind sie keine guten Aquariumpflanzen, weil sie das Licht blockieren, das die Aquariumpflanzen unter Wasser daher nicht erreichen kann. Die schwimmenden Pflanzen sind grundsätzlich Teichpflanzen, und dieser Abschnitt dient  nur dazu, Ihnen Pflanzen zu zeigen, die für Heimaquarien *nicht empfohlen* werden.

Schließlich gibt es einen dritten Abschnitt—*Erdpflanzen*—in dem Pflanzen aufgeführt sind, die keine Wasserpflanzen sind, aber manchmal trotzdem in Aquarien verwendet werden. Zweck dieses Abschnitts ist, Sie grundsätzlich darüber zu informieren, welche Pflanzen Sie *nicht* in Ihrem Aquarium verwenden sollten. Sie werden sterben. Aus diesem Grund finden Sie für jede Pflanzensorte in diesem Abschnitt nur ein kleines Foto und ihren Namen.

Alle Informationen in den übrigen Abschnitten dieser Hinweise für den Benutzer treffen nur auf den Abschnitt Echte Wasserpflanzen in diesem Buch zu.

## Anordnung der Seite

Auf den meisten Seite im Abschnitt *Echte Wasserpflanzen* befinden sich zwei Pflanzen. Neben dem Foto einer Pflanze und den jeweiligen Informationen erscheint eine Kennung, wie z.B. Ⓐ

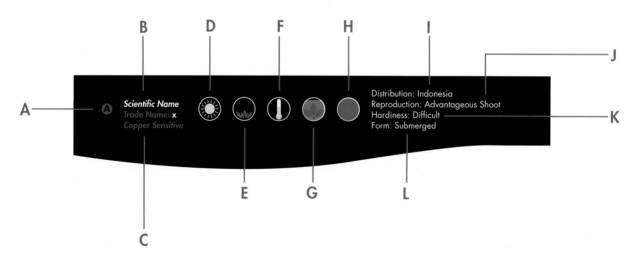

## Der Informationsbalken

Der Informationsbalken enthält Tatsachen über die Pflanzen in einem einfachen Format, die auf einen Blick ersichtlich sind. Nachstehend ein Beispiel eines Informationsbalkens. Die Symbole und der Text erscheinen stets in der gleichen Reihenfolge.

**A. Die Identifikation:** Der Nummernkennung ganz links im Balken entspricht einer Nummer neben einem der Pflanzenfotos auf der Seite. Diese Nummer verknüpft das Foto und die Informationen über diese Pflanze miteinander.

**B. Die Namenszeile:** Die drei Namenszeilen links im Informationsbalken enthalten (1) den wissenschaftlichen Namen der Pflanze (Gattung und Spezies), (2) einen gebräuchlichen Handelsnamen dieser Pflanze, und (3) Die Zeile kupferempfindlich.

**C. Die Zeile kupferempfindlich:** Diese orange Zeile — unter den Namenszeilen — erscheint nicht in jedem Eintrag. Sie ist nur zu sehen, wenn eine Pflanze *jegliche* Mengen Kupfer oder Kupfersulfat im Wasser nicht tolerieren kann.

# Hinweise Für Den Benutzer

**D. Symbol für Lichtanforderungen:** Unterschiedliche Pflanzen gedeihen unter unterschiedlichen Lichtbedingungen. Dieses Symbol informiert Sie über die *Mindest*-Lichtanforderungen jeder Pflanze. Die Symbole und ihre Bedeutung sind nachstehend abgebildet. Die Wattzahlen, die für die Lichtanforderungen aufgeführt sind, gelten für Aquarien mit einer Tiefe von 50 cm oder weniger. Außerdem handelt es sich bei den Wattzahlen, die für jedes Symbol aufgeführt sind, um die *Watt pro 3,78 Liter* mit Vollspektrum-Leuchtstoffröhren.

*Hell: 3.5 – 4.5 Watt*        *Mittel: 2.5 – 3.0 Watt*        *Niedrig: 1.5 – 2.0 Watt*

**E. Symbol für die Plazierung der Pflanzen:** Der Zweck dieses Symbols ist relativ leicht zu erkennen. Pflanzen können aufgrund ihrer Höhe und Struktur als Pflanzen im Vordergrund, Mittelgrund oder Hintergrund eingestuft werden. Zum Beispiel wird ein dünne, hohe Pflanze als eine Pflanze im *Hintergrund* eingestuft, und eine niedrige Pflanze, die den Boden bedeckt, als eine Pflanze im *Vordergrund* eingestuft.

*Vordergrund*        *Mittelgrund*        *Hintergrund*

**F. Temperatursymbol:** Dieses Symbol (natürlich ein Thermometer), gibt den idealen Temperaturbereich an, in dem eine Pflanze gedeihen wird. Es ist relativ wichtig, daß Sie dafür sorgen, daß das Wasser im Aquarium eine Temperatur innerhalb des Bereichs hat, der für diese Pflanze optimal ist — egal, welche Umweltbedingungen außerhalb des Aquarium herrschen. Die meisten Pflanzen fallen in den mittleren Temperaturbereich. Die verschiedenen Temperatursymbole und ihre Bedeutungen sind nachstehend abgebildet.

*Hoch: 29–30° Grad C*        *Mittel: 23–28° Grad C*        *Niedrig: 18–22° Grad C*

**G. Umweltsymbol:** Dieses Symbol teilt Ihnen mit, ob eine wirkliche Aquariumpflanze eine *Wasserpflanze* ist (d.h. sie kann gedeihen, wenn sie entweder vollständig oder teilweise unter Wasser ist) oder ob sie eine *Unterwasserpflanze* ist, die vollständig unter Wasser existieren kann.

*Unterwasserpflanze*        *Wasserpflanze*

**H. pH-Symbol:** Dieses Symbol gibt den optimalen pH-Wert für das Wachstum jeder Pflanzenspezies in Ihrem Aquarium an. Jeder farbige Kreis stellt einen unterschiedlichen pH-Wert dar. Die Symbole und ihre Bedeutungen sind nachstehend abgebildet:

*Alkalisch: 7,1–8,0 pH*        *Neutral: 7,0 pH*        *Sauer: 6,9–6,0 pH*

# Hinweise Für Den Benutzer

**I. Informationszeile über die Verbreitung:** Diese Zeile (die mit dem Wort *distribution* gekennzeichnet ist), teilt Ihnen mit, wo man diese Pflanze im allgemeinen in der Natur findet.

**J. Informationszeile über die Vermehrungsmethode:** Pflanzen vermehren sich auf verschiedene Arten. Diese Zeile (die mit dem Wort *reproduction* gekennzeichnet ist), informiert Sie darüber, welche Vermehrungsmethode jede Art verwendet:

> *Rhizome (Wurzelstock):* Pflanzen, die Schößling produzieren, die aus einem dicken, wurzelartigen Stamm sprießen. Die Wurzelstöcke können von der Hauptpflanze abgeschnitten und individuell eingepflanzt werden.

> *Bulb (Knolle):* Pflanzen, die von einer knolligen Basis aus wachsen, die Wurzeln nach unten und Blätter nach oben streckt.

> *Cutting (Ableger):* Pflanzen, die Wurzeln von Knötchen am Stengel der Hauptpflanze entwickeln. Sie können in eine neue Pflanze abgeteilt werden.

> *Adv. Shoot (vorteilhafter Schößling):* Die Mutterpflanze produziert blühende Schößlinge, die neue Pflanzen formen; außerdem können sich aus alten Blättern neue Pflanzen bilden.

> *Runners (Ausläufer):* Horizontale, kriechende Stengel, die sich von einer Pflanze ausstrecken und Schleicher (kleine, nußähnliche Knollen) besitzen, aus denen sich neue Pflanzen entwickeln.

> *Seeds & Spores (Samen und Sporen):* Diese Methode wird von Hobby-Aquarianern üblicherweise nicht benutzt, weil es normalerweise zu lange dauert, bis die Pflanzen ihre volle Größe erreicht haben.

**K. Informationszeile über die Widerstandsfähigkeit:** Diese Zeile (die mit dem Wort *hardiness* gekennzeichnet ist) sagt Ihnen, ob die Haltung einer bestimmten Pflanze im Aquarium *easy (leicht), moderate (mittelmäßig)* oder *difficult (schwierig)* ist. Sie sollten beachten, daß alle Pflanzen im Abschnitt *Terrariumpflanzen* in einem Aquarium praktisch zum Scheitern verurteilt sind.

**L. Informationszeile über die Form:** Diese Zeile (die mit dem Wort *form* gekennzeichnet ist) sagt Ihnen, ob die auf dem Foto abgebildet Pflanze *submerged (unter Wasser)* oder *emerged (außerhalb des Wassers)* gewachsen ist.

# Guide de l'utilisateur

## Structure de l'ouvrage

*Aquarium plants : The practical guide* est divisé en trois parties : les véritables plantes aquatiques, les plantes terrestres et les plantes flottantes. L'essentiel de ce livre se trouve dans la partie consacrée aux *véritables plantes aquatiques*. Un grand nombre d'informations est fourni pour chaque plante dans un format permettant la compréhension des informations d'un seul coup d'oeil ce tableau est appelé "barre d'information" et est expliqué dans le paragraphe qui lui est consacré.

Les *plantes flottantes* est un chapitre plus petit qui présente les véritables plantes aquatiques qui flottent à la surface de l'eau. Bien que ces plantes soient de véritables plantes aquatiques, elles ne sont pas du tout adaptées pour les aquariums, car elles empêchent la lumière de parvenir aux plantes totalement submergées situées au fond de l'aquarium.

Les plantes flottantes sont généralement mieux adaptées pour les bassins et ce chapitre présente des plantes que l'on peut placer dans des aquariums d'exposition et non des aquariums personnels.

Le troisième chapitre est consacré aux plantes terrestres qui ne sont pas aquatiques, mais que l'on trouve pourtant dans certains aquariums. Ce chapitre veut vous présenter les plantes qu'il ne faut pas utiliser dans l'aquarium parce qu'elles finissent par mourir. Une petite photo avec le nom de la plante illustre chaque variété.

Toutes les autres informations s'appliquent au chapitre consacré aux *véritables plantes aquatiques*.

## Organisation de la page

La plupart des pages du chapitre les *véritables plantes aquatiques* montrent deux plantes. Une étiquette, comme le Ⓐapparaîtra à côté de chaque photo de plante avec ses informations appropriées.

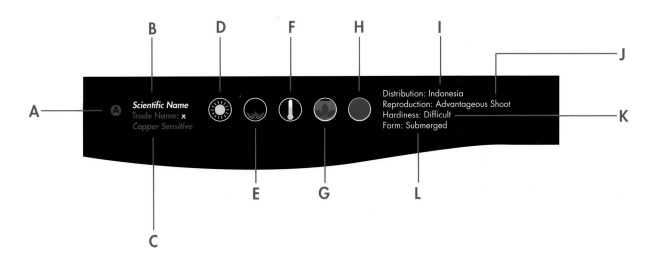

## La barre d'information

La barre d'information fournit les informations sur les plantes dans un format simple et perceptible d'un seul coup d'oeil. Un exemple de la barre d'informations est donné ci-dessous. Les icônes et le texte apparaîssent toujours dans le même ordre.

**A. L'étiquette d'information :** l'étiquette numérotée sur la gauche correspond au numéro de la photo d'une plante présentée sur cette page. Ce nombre associe la plante aux informations qui la concernent.

**B. La ligne d'identification :** les trois lignes d'identification situées à gauche de la barre d'information contiennent : 1-le nom scientifique de la plante (son genre et son espèce), 2-son appellation courante, 3-sensibilité au cuivre.

**B. La ligne de sensibilité au cuivre :** cette ligne orange située sous la ligne d'identification n'apparaît pas à chaque fois. Elle n'est présente que lorsqu'une plante ne tolère pas même une faible quantité de cuivre ou de sulfate de cuivre dans l'eau.

**D. L'icône des besoins lumineux :** les plantes selon leur variété croîssent sous des intensités lumineuses différentes. Cette icône vous informe des besoins minimums qu'ont chaque plante. Les autres icônes et leur signification sont présentées ci-dessous. La puissance en watts correspond pour des aquariums d'une hauteur d'eau d'environ 50 cm. Le rapport en watts donné pour chaque icône correspond à 1 watt pour 3,78 litres d'eau pour le spectre complet des tubes fluorescents.

*Large : 3.5-4.5 watts*    *Moyen: 2.5– 3.0 watts*    *Bas: 1.5– 2.0 watts*

**E. Icône de positionnement des plantes :** le sens de cette icône s'explique par lui-même. Les plantes sont classées en fonction de leur emplacement préférentiel dans l'aquarium : à l'avant-plan, au centre ou à l'arrière-plan et par rapport à leur taille et à leur structure. Par exemple, une plante fine et grande fera partie des plantes d'arrière-plan, tandis qu'une plante basse et épaisse fera partie des plantes d'avant-plan.

*Avant-plan*    *Centre*    *Arrière-plan*

**F. Icône de température :** Cette icône (un thermomètre, bien entendu !) indique la fourchette de température dans laquelle la plante aura une croissance correcte. Il est ensuite important de maintenir la température de l'eau de l'aquarium dans cette fourchette pour obtenir une bonne croissance. La plupart des plantes tombe dans une fourchette médiane. Les diverses icônes et leur signification sont indiqués ci-dessous :

*Elevé: 29– 30° C*    *Moyen: 23–28° C*    *Bas: 18–22° C*

**G. Icône d'environnement :** Cette icône indique si une plante est amphibie (si elle peut vivre partiellement immergée ou totalement) ou s'il s'agit d'une plante aquatique (qui vit constamment sous l'eau).

*Aquatique*    *Amphibie*

**H. L'icône du pH :** Cette icône indique dans quelle fourchette le pH de l'eau doit se trouver. Chaque disque coloré représente une fourchette de pH différent. Les diverses icônes et leur signification sont indiqués ci-dessous :

*Alcalin: pH 7.1–8.0*    *Neutre: pH 7.0*    *Acide: pH 6.9–6.0*

# Guide de l'utilisateur

**I. Ligne d'information sur la distribution :** Cette ligne (signalée par le mot *distribution*) vous informe de l'endroit où on trouve généralement la plante dans la nature.

**J. Ligne d'information sur les méthodes de reproduction :** Les plantes se reproduisent de façons très variées. Cette ligne (signalée par le mot *reproduction*) vous indique le type de reproduction de chaque variété.

>  *Rhizome (Rhizome):* Plantes qui produisent une tige souterraine portant des racines adventives. Les rhizomes de la plante-mère peuvent être sectionnés et plantés individuellement.

> *Bulbe (Bulb):* Plantes envoyant des racines vers le bas et des feuilles vers le haut à partir de leur bulbe.

> *Bouture (Cutting):* Plantes qui développent des racines à la base de leur tige. On peut les couper pour en faire de nouvelles plantes.

> *Rejetons (Adv. Shoot):* La plante-mère produit des rejetons qui peuvent former de nouvelles plantes. Les vieilles feuilles peuvent aussi former de nouvelles plantes.

> *Rampantes (Runners):* des tiges rampantes s'étendent et développent des stolons qui forment de nouvelles plantes.

> *Semis et spores (Seeds and Spores):* Cette méthode n'est pas souvent utilisée par les aquariophiles parce que les plantes prennent plus de temps pour se développer et atteindre une taille respectable.

**K. Ligne d'information de niveau de difficulté :** Cette ligne vous indique le niveau de difficulté (facile, moyen ou difficile) pour le maintien de certaines plantes en aquarium. Vous constaterez que les plantes présentées dans le chapitre sur les plantes de terrarium doivent être placées dans un aquarium.

**L. Ligne d'information sur la forme :** Cette ligne vous indique si la plante s'est développée sous l'eau ou hors de l'eau.

# Gids Voor De Gebruiker

## Samenstelling van het boek.

Aquariumplanten: "The Practical Guide" is onderverdeeld in drie hoofdstukken: De echte aquariumplanten, vaste planten en drijvende planten. Het grootste gedeelte van het boek handelt over de echte aquariumplanten. De meeste pagina's in dit onderdeel beschrijven twee planten. Er is een uitgebreide informatie per plant voorhanden die op een overzichtelijke manier wordt gegeven. Wij noemen het "informatiecode" en die wordt beschreven in de paragraaf "informatiecode" van deze gebruikersgids.

"Drijvende planten" is een kleiner hoofdstuk dat de meest voorkomende, echte waterplanten die aan de oppervlakte drijven, catalogeert. Hoewel het echte waterplanten zijn die in het water gedijen zijn het geen goede aquariumplanten omdat ze het licht beletten om de onderwaterplanten te bereiken. Drijvende planten zijn eigenlijk meer vijverplanten en dit hoofdstuk is er om aan te tonen dat dergelijke planten niet aan te raden zijn als aquariumbewoners.

Vaste planten tenslotte. Hier worden de planten gecatalogeerd die niet als waterplant kunnen fungeren maar toch soms in een aquarium worden gebruikt. De bedoeling van dit hoofdstuk is u te tonen welke planten in een aquarium niet hoeven gebruikt te worden: ze zullen afsterven. Daarom wordt van elke variëteit enkel de naam en
een kleine foto gegeven.

Alle informatie in de overige paragrafen van deze gebruikersgids heeft enkel betrekking op het onderdeel van dit boek :
"De echte aquariumplanten".

## Bladschikking

De meeste pagina's in het onderdeel "De echte aquariumplanten" behandelen twee planten. Een symbool, Ⓐ bv. staat naast de foto en de specifieke plantgegevens.

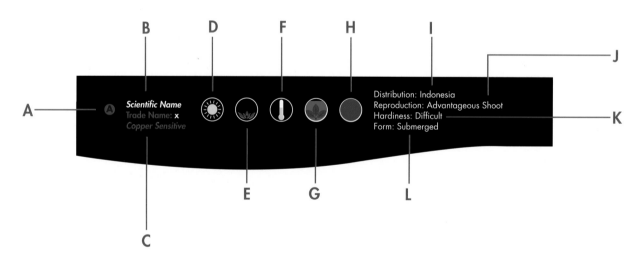

## De informatie code

De informatie code verstrekt u gegevens over de planten op een eenvoudige en overzichtelijke manier. Hieronder een voorbeeld van de informatie code. Beeld en tekst blijven steeds in dezelfde volgorde.

**A. Het identificatie label:** Het label aan de linkerkant van de code komt overeen met het nummer naast een van de foto's op de pagina. Dit nummer verbindt foto en informatie over de plant.

**B. De naam-lijn:** De drie namen links van de informatiecode behelst (1) de wetenschappelijke naam (soort en voorkomen), (2) de handelsnaam van de plant, (3) de kopergevoeligheid lijn.

**C. De kopergevoeligheid lijn:** Deze oranjekleurige lijn gesitueerd onder de naamlijn - komt niet overal voor. Ze wordt enkel getekend wanneer een plant geen enkele hoeveelheid koper of kopersulfaat in het water kan verdragen.

# Gids Voor De Gebruiker

**D. Lichtvereisten:** Zowat elke plant gedijt onder andere lichtomstandigheden. Deze figuren informeren u over de minimum hoeveelheid licht die elke plant nodig heeft. Deze figuren met wat ze voorstellen worden hieronder verduidelijkt. Het opgegeven aantal Watt, nodig voor voldoende licht, geldt voor aquaria van 50 cm hoogte (of minder). Voor elke figuur is het lichtvermogen gegeven in watt per 3.78 liter en dat voor fluorescerende lampen met een volledig lichtspectrum.

*Helder: 3.5–4.5 Watt*     *Medium: 2.5–3.0 Watt*     *Laag: 1.5–2.0 Watt*

**E. Plaats der planten:** De bedoeling van deze figuur is een totaal zelfontwerp mogelijk te maken. Planten kunnen gebruikt worden als voorgrond, middenin of als achtergond in functie van hun hoogte en vorm. Voorbeeld: Een ranke hoge plant zal als achtergrond fungeren terwijl planten die kort bij de grond blijven op de voorgrond dienen geplaatst.

*Voorgrond*     *Midden*     *Achtergrond*

**F. Temperatuur:** Deze figuur (een thermometer uiteraard) duidt de ideale temperatuur aan waarbij en plant het best zal groeien. Het is vrij belangrijk de temperatuur van uw aquarium te houden binnen deze grenzen die optimaal zijn voor die plant, wat ook de omgevingstemperatuur buiten het aquarium moge zijn. De meeste planten vallen zowat binnen een gemiddelde temperatuurswaarde. De diverse voorstellingen nopens de temperatuur kan u hieronder zien.

*Hoog: 29–30° C*     *Med: 23–28° C*     *Laag: 18–22° C*

**G. Omgeving:** Deze figuur vertelt u wanneer een echte aquariumplant een amfibie is (bedoeld wordt of ze kan groeien, helemaal of slechts gedeeltelijk onder water) dan wel een onderwaterplant, enkel in staat te overleven wanneer zij zich compleet onder water bevindt.

*Ondergedompeld*     *Amfibie*

**H. pH:** Deze figuur geeft de optimale pH-waarde voor de goede groei van elke plant. Elk gekleurd vakje betekent een andere pH-waarde. De figuren en hun betekenis kan u hieronder zien.

*Alkalisch: 7,1–8,0 pH*     *Neutraal: 7,0 pH*     *Zuur: 6,9–6,0 pH*

# Gids Voor De Gebruiker

**I. Herkomst:** Deze lijn (aangeduid met het woord "Distribution") geeft informatie over de plaats in de vrije natuur waar de plant meestal wordt gevonden.

**J. Kweekmetoden:** Planten zetten zich voort op verschillende manieren. Deze lijn (aangeduid met het woord "Reproduction") vertelt u hoe de voortplanting gebeurt voor elke variëteit:

> *Rhizome (wortelstokken):* planten die scheuten voortbrengen uit een dikke wortelstengel. De wortelstokken kunnen van de plant worden afgesneden en elders geplant. Bulb (knollen): de planten groeien uit knollen met wortels onderaan en bladeren bovenaan.

> *Cutting (scheuren of snijden):* Planten die wortels ontwikkelen uit knoesten op de stengel van de moederplant. Deze kunnen weggenomen worden om een nieuwe plant te vormen.

> *Adv. Shoot (bloeiaren):* de moederplant ontwikkelt bloeiende scheuten die nieuwe planten vormen. Ook kunnen nieuwe planten ontstaan uit bladeren van oude.

> *Runners (lopers):* De, van uit de moederplant, horizontaal uitdeinende wortels zijn voorzien van stola (knollen die lijken op kleine nootjes) waaruit zich nieuwe planten ontwikkelen.

> *Seeds & Spores (zaden en sporen):* Deze metode is niet gebruikelijk bij hobbyisten omdat de planten vaak een lange tijd nodig hebben om tot volle wasdom te komen.

**K. Hardheidsinformatie:** Deze lijn (aangeduid met het woord "Hardness") vertelt u of het al dan niet gemakkelijk (easy), matig (moderate) of moeilijk (difficult) is, om een dergelijke plant in een

aquarium te houden. Noteer goed dat alle planten uit het onderdeel Terrariumplanten, gegarandeerd veroordeeld zijn in een aquarium!

**L. Voorkomen:** Deze lijn (aangeduid met het woord "Form") vertelt u indien de plant op de foto volledig onder water groeide ("submerged") dan wel buiten het water ("emerged").

# True Aquatic Plants

plants. By this, I mean plants that can grow and thrive when permanently submerged. While all true aquatic plants can live under-water, many are *amphibious*: they are capable of living both in and out of the water.

Amphibious plants are able to live completely out of the water *provided that their root systems are constantly kept moist*. It is interesting to note that the submerged and emerged forms of the same variety of amphibious aquatic plants will often look different. This is due to differences in their environment. Most aquatic plants are fairly adaptable and can tolerate a wide range of water conditions (pH, dKH, dH). This is not to say that there aren't conditions that are better suited for various aquarium plants. Most of these plants grow best in soft, neutral, or slightly acidic water. In addition to not providing ideal conditions for many

calcium) can cause calcium sediments to coat the leaves and interfere with metabolic functions, including photosynthesis. Of course, providing conditions that promote sufficient photosynthesis is vitally important for keeping aquarium plants healthy. One of the most important elements for photosynthesis that you can provide is proper lighting. In this section, each plant's *minimum* light requirement is provided as an icon. I suggest that you choose the plants according to the light intensity that you can provide. You need to furnish enough illumination to accomodate those plants that have the highest light requirements. Plants that need lower light levels will not be harmed by more light, but the reverse is not true. In fact, provided that sufficient CO2 and nutrients are available, lower light plants will simply take advantage of the extra illumination and grow faster.

In diesem Abschnitt des Buchs befasse ich mich mit echten Wasserpflanzen. Hiermit meine ich Pflanzen, die wachsen und gedeihen können, wenn sie sich permanent unter Wasser befinden.

Obwohl alle echten Wasserpflanzen unter Wasser leben können, sind viele von ihnen Amphibienpflanzen: sie können sowohl im Wasser als auch außerhalb des Wassers leben. Amphibienpflanzen sind in der Lage, vollständig außerhalb des Wassers zu leben, vorausgesetzt, ihre Wurzelsysteme werden ständig feucht gehalten.

Es ist interessant, daß die Formen unter Wasser und außerhalb des Wassers der gleichen Art einer Amphibien-Wasserpflanze oft unterschiedlich aussehen. Dies ist auf die Unterschiede in ihrer Umwelt zurückzuführen. Die meisten Wasserpflanzen sind relativ anpassungsfähig und können ein breites Sortiment an Wasserbedingungen (pH, dKH, dH) tolerieren. Das heißt aber nicht, daß es nicht Bedingungen gibt, die besser für verschiedene Aquariumpflanzen geeignet sind. Generell wachsen die meisten dieser Pflanzen in weichem, neutralem oder leicht saurem Wasser am besten. Hartes Wasser (das zu viel Kalzium enthält) bietet vielen

Wasserpflanzen keine idealen Bedingungen und kann außerdem verursachen, daß die Blätter von Kalzium-ablagerungen überzogen und metabolische Funktionen einschließlich Photosynthese gestört werden. Um Aquariumpflanzen gesund zu erhalten, ist es natürlich lebenswichtig, daß für Bedingungen gesorgt wird, die eine ausreichende Photosynthese fördern.

Eines der wichtigsten Elemente für die Photosynthese, für das Sie sorgen können, ist die richtige Beleuchtung. In diesem Abschnitt wird die Mindest-Lichtanforderung jeder Pflanze mit einem Symbol dargestellt. Ich empfehle Ihnen, sich die Pflanzen gemäß der Lichtintensität auszusuchen, die Sie bieten können. Sie müssen für genügend Beleuchtung sorgen, um die Bedürfnisse der Pflanzen mit den höchsten Lichtanforderungen erfüllen zu können. Pflanzen, die niedrigere Lichtniveaus benötigen, werden durch mehr Licht nicht geschädigt, aber das Gegenteil trifft nicht zu. Tatsächlich werden Pflanzen, die weniger Licht benötigen die Extrabeleuchtung, so lange genügend $CO_2$ und Nährstoffe vorhanden sind, ausnutzen und schneller wachsen.

# Les Plantes Aquatiques ▪ Aquariumplanten

Dans cette partie du livre, je commente les véritables plantes aquatiques, c'est à dire les plantes qui peuvent se développer et pousser sous l'eau de façon permanente.

Il est intéressant de constater que parmi les véritables plantes aquatiques un certain nombre est amphibie. Tant que leur système de racines est constamment maintenu dans un milieu humide, leurs feuilles sont capables de passer de la vie aquatique à la vie terrestre sans aucun problème. Cependant, on observera souvent que la forme émergée et la forme immergée de la même variété de plante aquatique n'ont plus le même aspect. Cette modification est dûe à un environnement différent. La plupart des plantes aquatiques s'adaptent assez bien, et peuvent tolérer un large éventail de différentes qualités d'eau avec divers pH, dKH ou GH. Toutefois, il ne faut pas perdre de vue que certaines conditions conviennent mieux à certaines plantes. Généralement, la plupart de ces plantes se développent mieux dans une eau douce avec un pH neutre, voire légèrement acide. Une des conditions pour ne pas obtenir de belles plantes est d'employer une eau dure (contenant un taux excessif de calcium), car les sédiments calcaires peuvent alors recouvrir la surface des feuilles, et le fonctionnement du métabolisme de la plante ou même la photosynthèse s'en trouvent perturbés. Bien entendu, le fait de fournir des conditions permettant le bon déroulement de la photosynthèse est essentiel pour obtenir de belles plantes en bonne santé.

Un des éléments les plus importants contribuant à la photosynthèse est un éclairage adapté. Dans cette partie, les besoins minimaux de chaque plante sont indiqués dans une icone. Je suggère que vous choisissiez vos plantes en fonction de l'intensité lumineuse que vous comptez apporter.

Il vous faut apporter suffisamment d'énergie lumineuse aux plantes dont les besoins sont les plus importants. Un éclairage puissant n'abimera pas les plantes ayant des besoins plus modestes, mais procéder à l'inverse peut causer des dommages. En fait, il suffira d'approvisionnement régulièrement en CO2 et en engrais les plantes ayant de faibles besoins lumineux pour qu'elles grandissent bien plus vite.

In dit deel van het boek bespreek ik de echte waterplanten. Hiermee bedoel ik: planten die kunnen groeien en tot volle wasdom komen wanneer ze zich permanent onder water bevinden.

Hoewel alle echte waterplanten onder water kunnen leven hebben velen onder hen een amfibie-karakter: ze kunnen zowel in, als uit het water voorkomen. Dergelijke planten kunnen buiten het water leven op voorwaarde dat hun wortels constant vochtig blijven. Het is goed om weten dat van de z.g.n. amfibieplanten, de onderwater- en bovenwatervormen van dezelfde variëteit dikwijls verschillend lijken. Dit is te wijten aan de verschillen in hun omgeving.

De meeste waterplanten kunnen zich vrij goed aanpassen en verdragen een tamelijk brede spreiding in de watercondities (pH,dKH,dH). Hiermee hebben we niet gezegd dat er geen omstandigheden zijn die het best geschikt zijn voor de vele variëteiten der waterplanten. Als algemene regel geldt dat de meeste planten optimaal groeien in zacht, neutraal of licht-zuur water. Wanneer bijgevolg geen aandacht besteed wordt aan ideale condities dan kunnen de bladeren van veel waterplanten in hard water (met veel calcium) bedekt worden met een kalklaag en worden de stofwisselingsfuncties evenals de fotosynthese belemmerd. Het scheppen van omstandigheden die een efficiënte fotosynthese bevorderen is van levensbelang voor het gezond houden van aquariumplanten. Een van de belangrijkste elementen voor een goede fotosynthese is een degelijke belichting. De minimum behoefte aan licht voor iedere plant is een vast gegeven. Ik raad dus aan om planten te kiezen in functie van de hoeveelheid licht die je ze kan bezorgen. De belichting wordt dus gekozen in functie van de planten die de hoogste lichteisen stellen. Planten die minder licht nodig hebben ondervinden geen schade door een teveel aan licht: het omgekeerde is echter niet waar. Immers, bij aanwezigheid van voldoende $CO_2$ en voedingsstoffen zullen planten met lagere lichtbehoefte voordeel halen uit die hogere lichtwaarde en sneller groeien.

**B**

61

Hardiness: Medium
Form: Emerged

**B** *Ammannia senegalensis*

Distribution: South Africa
Reproduction: Cuttings
Hardiness: Medium
Form: Submerged

Hardiness: High
Form: Emerged

**B** *Anubias barteri* **v. "Angustifolia"**

Distribution: Tropical West Africa
Reproduction: Rhizome/Seeds
Hardiness: High
Form: Emerged

Ⓐ *Anubias barteri v. "Barteri"*

Distribution: Tropical West Africa
Reproduction: Rhizome/Seeds
Hardiness: High
Form: Emerged

Ⓑ *Anubias barteri v. "Barteri Variegated"*

Distribution: Domestic
Reproduction: Rhizome/Seeds
Hardiness: High
Form: Emerged

**A** *Anubias barteri* v. "Coffeefolia"

Distribution: Tropical West Africa
Reproduction: Rhizome/Seeds
Hardiness: High
Form: Emerged

**B** *Anubias barteri* v. "Nana"

Distribution: Tropical West Africa
Reproduction: Rhizome/Seeds
Hardiness: High
Form: Emerged

**A** Anubias barteri v. "Round Leaf"

Distribution: Tropical West Africa
Reproduction: Rhizome/Seeds
Hardiness: High
Form: Emerged

**B** Anubias sp. "Congensis"

Distribution: Tropical West Africa
Reproduction: Rhizome/Seeds
Hardiness: High
Form: Emerged

**C** Anubias x. "Emerald Heart"
Trade Name: **Emerald Heart**

Distribution: Domestic
Reproduction: Rhizome
Hardiness: High
Form: Emerged

**A** *Anubias* **x.** "Frazeri"
Trade Name: **Frazeri Anubias**

Distribution: Domestic
Reproduction: Rhizome
Hardiness: High
Form: Emerged

**B** *Anubias gigantea*

Distribution: Tropical West Africa
Reproduction: Rhizome/Seeds
Hardiness: High
Form: Emerged

**A** *Anubias gillettii*

Distribution: Tropical West Africa
Reproduction: Rhizome/Seeds
Hardiness: High
Form: Emerged

**B** *Anubias gracilis*

Distribution: Tropical West Africa
Reproduction: Rhizome/Seeds
Hardiness: High
Form: Emerged

**C** *Anubias heterophylla*

Distribution: Tropical West Africa
Reproduction: Rhizome/Seeds
Hardiness: High
Form: Emerged

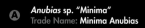    

**A**  *Anubias* sp. "Minima"
Trade Name: **Minima Anubias**

Distribution: Tropical West Africa
Reproduction: Seeds/Rhizome
Hardiness: High
Form: Emerged

**B**  *Anubias* sp. "Pygmy"
Trade Name: **Pygmy Anubias**

Distribution: West Africa
Reproduction: Rhizome
Hardiness: High
Form: Emerged

Hardiness: Medium
Form: Emerged

**B** *Anubias* sp. "Spade Leaf"
Trade Name: **Spade Leaf Anubias**

Distribution: Tropical West Africa
Reproduction: Rhizome
Hardiness: High
Form: Emerged

**A** Copper Sensitive

Hardiness: Medium
Form: Submerged

**B** *Aponogeton capuronii*
Copper Sensitive

Distribution: Madagascar
Reproduction: Bulbs/Seeds
Hardiness: Medium
Form: Submerged

**A** *Aponogeton crispus*
Trade Name: **Crispus**
*Copper Sensitive*

Distribution: Sri Lanka
Reproduction: Bulbs/Seeds
Hardiness: Medium
Form: Submerged

**B** *Aponogeton longiplumulosus*
*Copper Sensitive*

Distribution: Madagascar
Reproduction: Bulbs/Seeds
Hardiness: Medium
Form: Submerged

*Aponogeton madagascariensis*
A  Trade Name: **Madagascar Lace Plant**
   *Copper Sensitive*

Distribution: Madagascar
Reproduction: Bulbs/Seeds
Hardiness: Low
Form: Submerged

*Aponogeton madagascariensis* v. "Henkelianus"
B  Trade Name: **Henkelianus Lace Plant**
   *Copper Sensitive*

Distribution: Madagascar
Reproduction: Bulbs/Seeds
Hardiness: Low
Form: Submerged

Ⓐ Trade Name: **West Coast Madagascar Lace Plant**
   *Copper Sensitive*

Reproduction: Bulbs/Seeds
Hardiness: Low
Form: Submerged

Ⓑ *Aponogeton sp. "Madagascar"*
   *Copper Sensitive*

Distribution: Madagascar
Reproduction: Bulbs
Hardiness: Low
Form: Submerged

**A** Copper Sensitive
Hardiness: Medium
Form: Submerged

**B** *Aponogeton rigidifolius*
Copper Sensitive

Distribution: Sri Lanka
Reproduction:Rhizome/Seeds
Hardiness: Medium
Form: Submerged

Copper Sensitive

Hardiness: Low
Form: Submerged

B **Aponogeton undulatus**
*Copper Sensitive*

Distribution: India
Reproduction: Bulbs/Adv. Shoot
Hardiness: Medium
Form: Submerged

A **Bacopa caroliniana**      Hardiness: Medium
Form: Emerged

B **Bacopa caroliniana** Distribution: Southern United States
Reproduction: Cuttings/Seeds
Hardiness: Medium
Form: Submerged

A **Bacopa lanigera**

Distribution: Brazil
Reproduction: Cuttings/Seeds
Hardiness: Difficult
Form: Emerged

B **Bacopa monnieri**
Trade Name: **Money Wort**

Distribution: Tropical and Subtropical
America, Asia, Africa & Australia.
Reproduction: Cuttings/Seeds/Plantlets
Hardiness: Difficult
Form: Submerged

**Ⓐ** *Bacopa myriophylloides*

Distribution: Brazil
Reproduction: Cuttings/Seeds
Hardiness: Medium
Form: Emerged

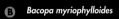    

**Ⓑ** *Bacopa myriophylloides*

Distribution: Brazil
Reproduction: Cuttings/Seeds
Hardiness: Medium
Form: Submerged

***Barclaya longifolia* v. "Red"**
**B** Trade Name: **Red Barclaya**
*Copper Sensitive*

Distribution: Southeast Asia
Reproduction: Bulbs/Seeds
Hardiness: Low
Form: Submerged

A
Copper Sensitive
Reproduction: Seeds
Hardiness: Low
Form: Submerged

B *Blyxa japonica*
Copper Sensitive
Reproduction: Seeds
Hardiness: Low
Form: Submerged

*Bolbitis heteroclita*
Trade Name: **El Niño Fern**
*Copper Sensitive*

Distrib.: Asia (India, Japan, New Guinae)
Reproduction: Rhizome
Hardiness: High
Form: Emerged

83

**Bolbitis heudelotii**
*Copper Sensitive*

Distribution: Africa
Reproduction: Rhizome
Hardiness: High
Form: Submerged

Copper Sensitive

Hardiness: Low
Form: Submerged

**B** *Cabomba caroliniana*

Distribution: U.S. and S. America
Reproduction: Cuttings
Hardiness: Medium
Form: Submerged

A

B

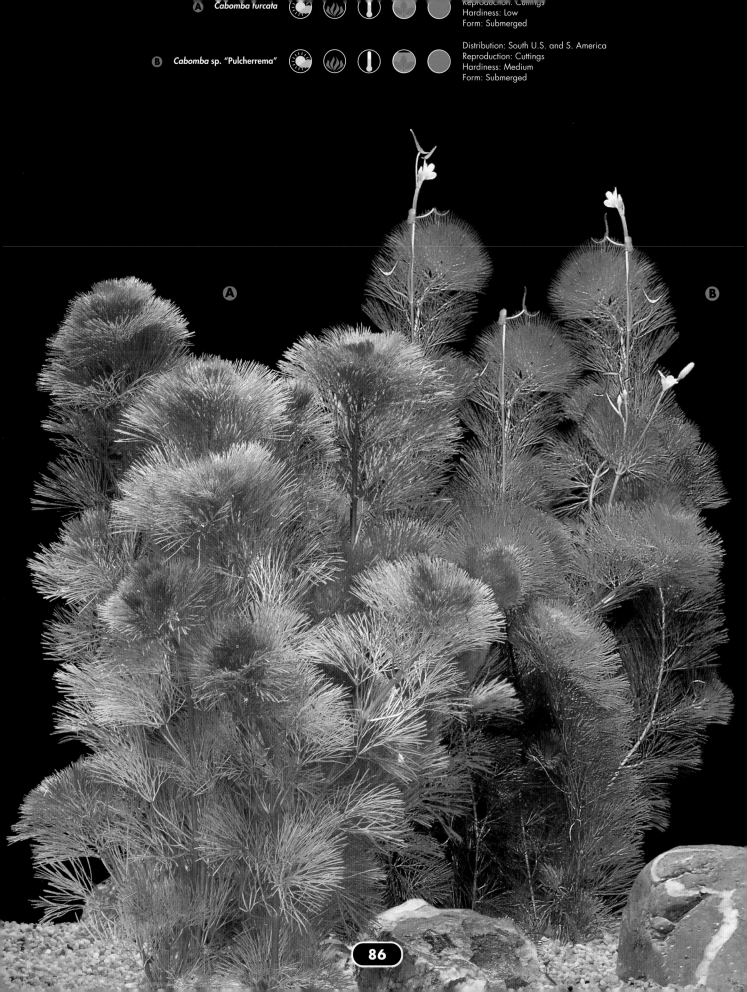

**A** *Cabomba furcata*

Reproduction: Cuttings
Hardiness: Low
Form: Submerged

**B** *Cabomba* sp. "Pulcherrema"

Distribution: South U.S. and S. America
Reproduction: Cuttings
Hardiness: Medium
Form: Submerged

**Ⓐ** *Cardamine lyrata*

Distribution: China and Japan
Reproduction: Cuttings
Hardiness: Low
Form: Submerged

**Ⓑ** *Ceratophyllum demersum*
Trade Name: **Hornwort**

Distribution: Worldwide
Reproduction: Cuttings
Hardiness: High
Form: Submerged

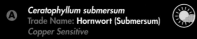 **A** *Ceratophyllum submersum*
Trade Name: **Hornwort (Submersum)**
*Copper Sensitive*

Distribution: Worldwide
Reproduction: Cuttings
Hardiness: Medium
Form: Submerged

**B** *Ceratophyllum pteridoides*
Trade Name: **Water Sprite (Pteridoides)**

Reproduction: Spore/Adv. Shoot
Hardiness: Medium
Form: Emerged

**A** *Ceratopteris thalictroides*
Trade Name: **Water Sprite**

Distribution: South Asia, Northern Australia
Reproduction: Adv. Shoot
Hardiness: Medium
Form: Emerged

**B** *Crassula helmsii*
*Copper Sensitive*

Distribution: Australia, New Zeland
Reproduction: Cuttings
Hardiness: Medium
Form: Submerged

**C** *Crinum calamistratum*

Distribution: West Africa
Reproduction: Bulbs/Seeds
Hardiness: High
Form: Submerged

**A** *Crinum natans*

Distribution: West Africa
Reproduction: Bulbs/Seeds
Hardiness: High
Form: Submerged

**B** *Crinum thaianum*
Trade Name: **Onion Plant**

Distribution: Southern Thailand
Reproduction: Bulbs/Seeds
Hardiness: High
Form: Submerged

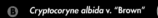 **_Cryptocoryne albida_ v. "Brown"**

Distribution: South Thailand
Reproduction: Seeds/Runners
Hardiness: Medium
Form: Emerged

Cryptocoryne albida v. 'Green'

Hardiness: Medium
Form: Emerged

**B** *Cryptocoryne amicorum*
*Copper Sensitive*

Distribution: Sumatra
Reproduction: Seeds/Rhizome/Runners
Hardiness: Low
Form: Emerged

Trade Name: **Blassii (Broad Leaf)**

Hardiness: Medium
Form: Submerged

Distribution: Sri Lanka
Reproduction: Seeds/Runners
Hardiness: Medium
Form: Submerged

B  *Cryptocoryne beckettii*

Cryptocoryne blassii v. Narrow Leaf
Trade Name: **Blassii (Narrow Leaf)**

Distribution: Malaysia
Reproduction: Seeds/Runners
Hardiness: Medium
Form: Submerged

 Cryptocoryne ciliata

Distribution: India
Reproduction: Seeds/Runners
Hardiness: Medium
Form: Emerged

Cryptocoryne cordata
Hardiness: Medium
Form: Submerged

Distribution: Southeast Asia
Reproduction: Seeds/Runners
Hardiness: Medium
Form: Submerged

**B** *Cryptocoryne crispatula* **v. "Balansae Brown"**

Ⓐ *Cryptocoryne crispatula* v. **Balansae Green**

Hardiness: Medium
Form: Submerged

Ⓑ *Cryptocoryne crispatula* v. **"Tonkenesis"**

Distribution: Southeast Asia
Reproduction: Seeds/Runners
Hardiness: Medium
Form: Submerged

**A** *Cryptocoryne gasseri*
*Copper Sensitive*

Reproduction: Seeds/Runners
Hardiness: Low
Form: Submerged

**B** *Cryptocoryne griffithii*
*Copper Sensitive*

Distribution: Malaysia
Reproduction: Seeds/Runners
Hardiness: Medium
Form: Submerged

Reproduction: Runners
Hardiness: Medium
Form: Submerged

**B** *Cryptocoryne lingua*
*Copper Sensitive*

Distribution: Borneo
Reproduction: Seeds/Runners
Hardiness: Medium
Form: Emerged

A **Cryptocoryne longicauda**

Reproduction: Seeds/Runners
Hardiness: Medium
Form: Emerged

A

B **Cryptocoryne moehlmannii**
*Copper Sensitive*

Distribution: Sumatra
Reproduction: Seeds/Runners
Hardiness: Medium
Form: Submerged

B

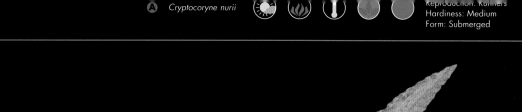

A

Ⓑ  *Cryptocoryne parva*

Distribution: Sri Lanka
Reproduction: Seeds/Runners
Hardiness: Medium
Form: Emerged

B

**(A)** *Cryptocoryne petchii*

Hardiness: Medium
Form: Emerged

**(B)** *Cryptocoryne petchii*

Distribution: Sri Lanka
Reproduction: Seeds/Runners
Hardiness: Medium
Form: Submerged

*Cryptocoryne spiralis*

Hardiness: Medium
Form: Emerged

*Cryptocoryne spiralis*

Distribution: Southern India
Reproduction: Seeds/Runners
Hardiness: Medium
Form: Submerged

**A** *Cryptocoryne striolata*

Distribution: Borneo
Reproduction: Seeds/Runners
Hardiness: Medium
Form: Submerged

**A**

**B** *Cryptocoryne sulphurea*

Distribution: Sumatra
Reproduction: Seeds/Runners
Hardiness: Medium
Form: Submerged

**B**

A *Cryptocoryne undulata*

Distribution: Sri Lanka
Reproduction: Seeds/Runners
Hardiness: Medium
Form: Submerged

B *Cryptocoryne usteriana*

Distribution: Philippines
Reproduction: Seeds/Runners
Hardiness: Medium
Form: Submerged

**B** *Cryptocoryne walkeri*

Distribution: Sri Lanka
Reproduction: Seeds/Runners
Hardiness: Medium
Form: Emerged

*Cryptocoryne wendtii* v. "Bronze"
Trade Name: **Bronze Wendtii**

Distribution: Sri Lanka
Reproduction: Seeds/Runners
Hardiness: Medium
Form: Emerged

**A** *Cryptocoryne wendtii* v. "Bronze"
Trade Name: **Bronze Wendtii**

Distribution: Sri Lanka
Reproduction: Seeds/Runners
Hardiness: Medium
Form: Submerged

**B** *Cryptocoryne wendtii* v. "Brown"
Trade Name: **Brown Wendtii**

Distribution: Sri Lanka
Reproduction: Seeds/Runners
Hardiness: Medium
Form: Emerged

**A** *Cryptocoryne wendtii* v. "Copper"
Trade Name: **Copper Wendtii**

Distribution: Sri Lanka
Reproduction: Seeds/Runners
Hardiness: Medium
Form: Emerged

**B** *Cryptocoryne wendtii* v. "Green"
Trade Name: **Green Wendtii**

Distribution: Sri Lanka
Reproduction: Seeds/Runners
Hardiness: Medium
Form: Submerged

**A** *Cryptocoryne wendtii* v. "Red"  Distribution: Sri Lanka
Reproduction: Seeds/Runners
Hardiness: Medium
Form: Emerged

**B** *Cryptocoryne wendtii* v. "Red"  Distribution: Sri Lanka
Reproduction: Seeds/Runners
Hardiness: Medium
Form: Submerged

**A** *Cryptocoryne wendtii* v. "Red Vein"

Hardiness: Medium
Form: Emerged

Distribution: Sri Lanka
Reproduction: Seeds/Runners
Hardiness: Medium
Form: Emerged

**B** *Cryptocoryne wendtii* v. "Rose"

A

 **Cryptocoryne wendtii** v. "Striped"
Trade Name: **Striped Wendtii**

Distribution: Sri Lanka
Reproduction: Seeds/Runners
Hardiness: Medium
Form: Emerged

B

Trade Name: **Striped Wendtii**

Hardiness: Medium
Form: Submerged

**B** *Didiplis diandra*

Distribution: Eastern North America
Reproduction: Seeds/Cuttings
Hardiness: Medium
Form: Submerged

A

B

**Echinodorus amazonicus**
Trade Name: **Amazon Sword Plant**

Reproduction: Rhizome/ Seeds/ Adv. Shoot
Hardiness: Medium
Form: Emerged

B **Echinodorus x. "Apart"**

Distribution: Domestic
Reproduction: Rhizome
Hardiness: Medium
Form: Submerged

*Echinodorus aschersonianus*

Hardiness: Medium
Form: Submerged

**B** *Echinodorus* x. "Barthii"
Trade Name: **Red Mellon**
*Copper Sensitive*

Distribution: Domestic
Reproduction: Rhizome
Hardiness: Medium
Form: Emerged

Trade Name: **Cellophane Sword Plant**
*Copper Sensitive*

Hardiness: Medium
Form: Submerged

**B** *Echinodorus bleheri*
Trade Name: **Amazon Sword Plant (Bleheri)**

Reproduction: Rhizome/Seeds/Adv. Shoot
Hardiness: Medium
Form: Emerged

*Echinodorus bleheri* v. "Robustus"
Trade Name: **Robustus Amazon Sword Plant**
Hardiness: Medium
Form: Emerged

**B** *Echinodorus bleheri* v. "Ruffled"
Trade Name: **Ruffled Amazon Sword Plant**
Reproduction: Rhizome/Adv. Shoot
Hardiness: Medium
Form: Emerged

*Echinodorus bolivianus*

Reproduction: Adv. Shoot
Hardiness: Medium
Form: Submerged

*Echinodorus cordifolius*
Trade Name: **Radican Sword Plant**

Distribution: North and South America
Reproduction: Rhizome/Seeds/Adv. Shoot
Hardiness: Medium
Form: Emerged

*Echinodorus cordifolius* v. "Tropica Marble Queen"
Trade Name: **Tropica Marble Queen**

Distribution: Domestic
Reproduction: Rhizome/Seeds/Adv. Shoot
Hardiness: Medium
Form: Emerged

*Echinodorus horizontalis*
Hardiness: Medium
Form: Emerged

**B** *Echinodorus horizontalis*

Distribution: South America
Reproduction: Rhizome/Seeds/Adv. Shoot
Hardiness: Medium
Form: Submerged

**Echinodorus x. "Indian Red"**
Trade Name: **Indian Red**
*Copper Sensitive*

Reproduction: Rhizome
Hardiness: Medium
Form: Submerged

**Echinodorus martii**
Trade Name: **Ruffled Sword Plant**
*Copper Sensitive*

Distribution: Brazil
Reproduction: Rhizome/Seeds/Adv. Shoot
Hardiness: Medium
Form: Emerged

***Echinodorus martii*** v. "Florida Aquatic"
*Copper Sensitive*

Reproduction: Rhizome/Adv. Shoot
Hardiness: Medium
Form: Emerged

***Echinodorus martii*** v. "Florida Aquatic"
*Copper Sensitive*

Distribution: Domestic
Reproduction: Rhizome/Adv. Shoot
Hardiness: Medium
Form: Submerged

**A** Trade Name: **Oriental Sword Plant**
*Copper Sensitive*

Hardiness: Medium
Form: Emerged

*Echinodorus* x. "Oriental"
**B** Trade Name: **Oriental Sword Plant**
*Copper Sensitive*

Distribution: Domestic
Reproduction: Rhizome/Adv. Shoot
Hardiness: Medium
Form: Submerged

Trade Name: **Mellon Sword Plant**
*Copper Sensitive*

Hardiness: Medium
Form: Emerged

**B** *Echinodorus osiris* v. "Variegated"
Trade Name: **Marbled Mellon Sword Plant**
*Copper Sensitive*

Distribution: Domestic
Reproduction: Rhizome/Adv. Shoot
Hardiness: Medium
Form: Emerged

 Trade Name: **Ozelot Sword Plant**
*Copper Sensitive*

Hardiness: Medium
Form: Emerged

*Echinodorus* x. "Ozelot"
 Trade Name: **Ozelot Sword Plant**
*Copper Sensitive*

Distribution: Domestic
Reproduction: Rhizome/Adv. Shoot
Hardiness: Medium
Form: Submerged

Trade Name: **Marble Ozelot Sword**
*Copper Sensitive*

Reproduction: Rhizome/Adv. Shoot
Hardiness: Medium
Form: Emerged

*Echinodorus* **x. "Ozelot Nova"**
Trade Name: **Nova Ozelot Sword**
*Copper Sensitive*

Distribution: Domestic
Reproduction: Rhizome/Adv. Shoot
Hardiness: Medium
Form: Submerged

Echinodorus parviflorus *Tropica*
Trade Name: **Tropica Parviflorus**

Reproduction: Rhizome/Seeds/Adv. Shoot
Hardiness: Medium
Form: Emerged

B  *Echinodorus portoalegrensis*
   *Copper Sensitive*

Distribution: Southern Brazil
Reproduction: Rhizome/Adv. Shoot
Hardiness: Difficult
Form: Submerged

Ⓐ Trade Name: **Broad Leaf Chain Sword**
*Copper Sensitive*

Hardiness: Medium
Form: Submerged

Ⓑ *Echinodorus* sp. "Rigidifolius"
*Copper Sensitive*

Distribution: South America
Reproduction: Rhizome
Hardiness: Medium
Form: Emerged

130

**A** *Echinodorus* x. "Rose"
*Copper Sensitive*

Distribution: Domestic
Reproduction: Rhizome/Adv. Shoot
Hardiness: Medium
Form: Emerged

**B** *Echinodorus* x. "Rose"
*Copper Sensitive*

Distribution: Domestic
Reproduction: Rhizome/Adv. Shoot
Hardiness: Medium
Form: Submerged

**A** *Echinodorus x. "Rubin"*
Trade Name: **Red Rubin**
*Copper Sensitive*

Distribution: Domestic
Reproduction: Rhizome/Adv. Shoot
Hardiness: Medium
Form: Emerged

**B** *Echinodorus x. "Rubin"*
Trade Name: **Red Rubin**
*Copper Sensitive*

Distribution: Domestic
Reproduction: Rhizome/Adv. Shoot
Hardiness: Medium
Form: Submerged

**A**  *Echinodorus* sp. "Scaber"   Reproduction: Rhizome/Adv. Shoot
Hardiness: Medium
Form: Emerged

**B**  *Echinodorus schlueteri*   Reproduction: Rhizome/Adv. Shoot
Hardiness: Medium
Form: Emerged

 **Echinodorus schlueteri v. "Leopard"**
Trade Name: **Leopard Radican**

Distribution: Domestic
Reproduction: Rhizome/Adv. Shoot
Hardiness: Medium
Form: Emerged

**Echinodorus subulatus**

Distribution: Central & South America
Reproduction: Rhizome/Adv. Shoot
Hardiness: Medium
Form: Emerged

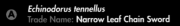

**A** *Echinodorus tennellus*
Trade Name: **Narrow Leaf Chain Sword**

Distribution: Central & South America
Reproduction: Seeds/Adv. Shoot
Hardiness: Medium
Form: Emerged

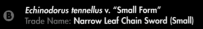

**B** *Echinodorus tennellus* v. "Small Form"
Trade Name: **Narrow Leaf Chain Sword (Small)**

Distribution: Central & South America
Reproduction: Seeds/Adv. Shoot
Hardiness: Medium
Form: Emerged

**C** *Echinodorus uruguayensis*
*Copper Sensitive*

Distribution: Uruguay, Chile, S. Brazil
Reproduction: Rhizome/Adv. Shoot
Hardiness: Medium
Form: Submerged

**Echinodorus uruguayensis v. "Green"**
(A) Trade Name: **Green Hormanii**
*Copper Sensitive*

Distribution: Uruguay, Chile, Argentina
Reproduction: Rhizome/Adv. Shoot
Hardiness: Medium
Form: Submerged

**Echinodorus uruguayensis v. "Red"**
(B) Trade Name: **Red Hormanii**
*Copper Sensitive*

Distribution: Uruguay, Chile, Argentina
Reproduction: Rhizome/Adv. Shoot
Hardiness: Medium
Form: Submerged

**Egeria najas**
Copper Sensitive

Distribution: South America
Reproduction: Seeds/Cuttings
Hardiness: Medium
Form: Submerged

Copper Sensitive

Hardiness: Medium
Form: Submerged

**B** *Eichhornia*
*diversifolia*
Copper Sensitive

Distribution: Central & South America
Reproduction: Seeds/Cuttings
Hardiness: Medium
Form: Submerged

**C** *Eleocharis acicularis*
Trade Name: **Dwarf Hairgrass**

Distribution: Worldwide
Reproduction: Runners
Hardiness: Medium
Form: Submerged

**A** *Eleocharis montevidensis*
Trade Name: **Giant Hairgrass**
Hardiness: Medium
Form: Emerged

**B** *Eleocharis vivipara*
Trade Name: **Hairgrass**
Distribution: Southern U.S.A
Reproduction: Adv. Shoot
Hardiness: High
Form: Emerged

**A** Copper Sensitive

Hardiness: Medium
Form: Submerged

**B** *Eusteralis stellata*
Copper Sensitive

Distribution: Malaysia, Japan, China, Taiwan
Reproduction: Seeds/Cuttings
Hardiness: Low
Form: Submerged

**C** *Fontinalis antipyretica*
Trade Name: **Willow Moss**

Distribution: Southeast U.S.A
Reproduction: Cuttings
Hardiness: Medium
Form: Submerged

**A** *Glossostigma elatinoides*
*Copper Sensitive*

Reproduction: Runners/Cuttings
Hardiness: Medium
Form: Emerged

**B** *Gymnocoronis spilanthoides*

Distribution: South America
Reproduction: Seeds/Cuttings
Hardiness: Medium
Form: Emerged

**C** *Gymnocoronis spilanthoides* v. "Variegated"

Distribution: Domestic
Reproduction: Seeds/Cuttings
Hardiness: Medium
Form: Emerged

**A** *Hemianthus micranthemoides*
Hardiness: Medium
Form: Submerged

**B** *Heteranthera zosterifolia*
*Copper Sensitive*
Distribution: Brazil, Uruguay, Argentina
Reproduction: Seeds/Cuttings
Hardiness: Medium
Form: Submerged

**C** *Hottonia palustris*
*Copper Sensitive*
Distribution: Europe, North Asia
Reproduction: Seeds/Cuttings
Hardiness: Medium
Form: Emerged

*Hydrocotyle leucocephala*
Trade Name: **Brazilian Pennywort**

Distribution: Central America & South America
Reproduction: Cuttings
Hardiness: Medium
Form: Emerged

*Hydrocotyle sibthorpioides*

Hardiness: Medium
Form: Emerged

B   *Hydrocotyle verticillata*
Trade Name: **Pennywort**

Distribution: Southeast U.S.A
Reproduction: Seeds/Cuttings
Hardiness: Medium
Form: Emerged

Hardiness: Medium
Form: Submerged

B *Hygrophila* **sp. "Asian"**

Distribution: Southeast Asia
Reproduction: Cuttings
Hardiness: Medium
Form: Emerged

A

B

**B** *Hygrophila corymbosa* x. "Greta"
Trade Name: **Greta Corymbosa**

Distribution: Domestic
Reproduction: Cuttings
Hardiness: Medium
Form: Emerged

Hygrophila corymbosa x. "Rune Leaf"

Hardiness: Medium
Form: Emerged

**B** *Hygrophila corymbosa* v. "Siamensis"
Trade Name: **Giant Hygro**

Distribution: Southeast Asia
Reproduction: Seeds/Cuttings
Hardiness: Medium
Form: Emerged

*Hygrophila corymbosa v. "Siamensis Broadleaf"*
Trade Name: **Broad Leaf Giant Hygro**

Distribution: Southeast Asia
Reproduction: Seeds/Cuttings
Hardiness: Medium
Form: Emerged

*Hygrophila corymbosa v.* "Siamensis Narrow Leaf"
Trade Name: **Narrow Leaf Giant Hygro**

Reproduction: Seeds/Cuttings
Hardiness: Medium
Form: Emerged

**B** *Hygrophila corymbosa v.* "Stricta"
Trade Name: **Temple Plant**

Distribution: Southeast Asia
Reproduction: Seeds/Cuttings
Hardiness: Medium
Form: Emerged

149

*Hygrophila col ymbosa* x. "Willow Leaf"
Hardiness: Medium
Form: Emerged

B  **Hygrophila difformis**
Trade Name: **Water Wisteria**

Distribution: India & Southeast Asia
Reproduction: Cutting
Hardiness: Medium
Form: Submerged

*Hygrophila difformis* V. Variegated
Trade Name: **Variegated Water Wisteria**

Reproduction: Cuttings
Hardiness: Medium
Form: Submerged

B
*Hygrophila polysperma*
Trade Name: **Hygro**

Distribution: India
Reproduction: Cutting
Hardiness: Medium
Form: Submerged

A

B

**Hygrophila polysperma** "Tropic Sunset"
Trade Name: **Tropic Sunset Hygro**

Reproduction: Cuttings
Hardiness: Medium
Form: Submerged

**B** *Hygrophila* sp. "Red"

Reproduction: Cutting
Hardiness: Medium
Form: Emerged

Trade Name: **Quillwort**

Hardiness: Medium
Form: Submerged

*Juncus repens*
Trade Name: **Palm Grass**

Distribution: Southeast U.S.A
Reproduction: Seeds/Cuttings
Hardiness: Medium
Form: Submerged

Copper Sensitive

Hardiness: Medium
Form: Submerged

**B**  *Lagenandra erosa*

Distribution: Sri Lanka
Reproduction: Rhizome
Hardiness: Medium
Form: Emerged

**A** *Lagenandra ovata*

Distribution: Sri Lanka
Reproduction: Rhizome
Hardiness: Medium
Form: Emerged

**B** *Lagenandra thawaitesii*

Distribution: Sri Lanka
Reproduction: Rhizome
Hardiness: Medium
Form: Emerged

**A** *Lemna trisulca*
Trade Name: **Chain of Stars**

Distribution: Worldwide
Reproduction: Cuttings
Hardiness: Medium
Form: Submerged

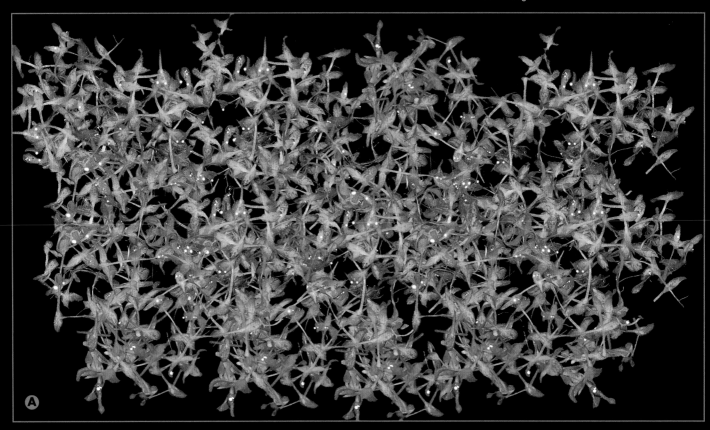

**B** *Lilaeopsis brasiliensis*
Trade Name: **Microsword**

Distribution: Brazil, Paraguay, Argentina
Reproduction: Runners
Hardiness: Medium
Form: Emerged

**B** *Limnophila aromatica*

Distribution: South Asia
Reproduction: Seeds/Cuttings
Hardiness: Medium
Form: Emerged

**(A) Limnophila heterophylla**

Reproduction: Seeds/Cuttings
Hardiness: Medium
Form: Submerged

**(B) Limnophila indica**

Distribution: Africa, Asia & Australia
Reproduction: Seeds/Cuttings
Hardiness: Medium
Form: Submerged

 **A** *Limnophila sessiliflora*

Distribution: Asia, India & Japan
Reproduction: Cuttings
Hardiness: Medium
Form: Emerged

 **B** *Limnophila sessiflora*

Distribution: Asia, India & Japan
Reproduction: Cuttings
Hardiness: Medium
Form: Submerged

**A** *Lindernia rotundifolia*

Distribution: Southeast U.S.A
Reproduction: Seeds/Cuttings
Hardiness: Medium
Form: Emerged

**B** *Lobelia cardinalis*

Distribution: Southeast U.S.A
Reproduction: Seeds/Cuttings
Hardiness: Medium
Form: Emerged

**B** *Ludwigia glandulosa*

Distribution: North America
Reproduction: Seeds/Cuttings
Hardiness: Medium
Form: Emerged

**A**

**B**

Trade Name: **Broad Leaf Lud**

Hardiness: Medium
Form: Emerged

**B** *Ludwigia repens* x. "Palustris"
Trade Name: **Broad Leaf Lud**

Distribution: U.S.A & Mexico
Reproduction: Seeds/Cuttings
Hardiness: Medium
Form: Submerged

Trade Name: **Pond Penny**

Hardiness: Medium
Form: Emerged

Ⓑ *Lysimachia nummularia* v. "Aurea"
Trade Name: **Aurea Pond Penny**

Distribution: Domestic
Reproduction: Seeds/Cuttings
Hardiness: Medium
Form: Emerged

Ⓐ *Mayaca fluviatilis*
Hardiness: Medium
Form: Submerged

Ⓑ *Micranthemum umbrosum*
*Copper Sensitive*
Distribution: United States
Reproduction: Seeds/Cuttings
Hardiness: Medium
Form: Emerged

Ⓒ *Micromeria brownei*
Trade Name: **Creeping Charlie**
Reproduction: Seeds/Cuttings
Hardiness: Medium
Form: Emerged

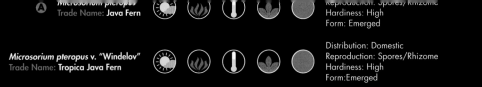

**A** *Microsorium pteropus*
Trade Name: **Java Fern**

Hardiness: High
Form: Emerged

**B** *Microsorium pteropus* v. "Windelov"
Trade Name: **Tropica Java Fern**

Distribution: Domestic
Reproduction: Spores/Rhizome
Hardiness: High
Form:Emerged

Trade Name: **Parrot's Feather**

Hardiness: Medium
Form: Emerged

B **Myriophyllum aquaticum**
Trade Name: **Parrot's Feather**

Distribution: South America
Reproduction: Cuttings
Hardiness: Medium
Form: Submerged

Trade Name: **Red Foxtail**

Hardiness: Medium
Form: Submerged

**(B)** *Myriophyllum pinnatum*
Trade Name: **Green Foxtail**

Distribution: North America
Reproduction: Cuttings
Hardiness: Medium
Form: Submerged

*Myriophyllum simulans*
Trade Name: **Filligree Myrio**

Distribution: Australia
Reproduction: Cuttings
Hardiness: Medium
Form: Submerged

*Myriophyllum tuberculatum*

Distribution: Brazil & Peru
Reproduction: Cuttings
Hardiness: Medium
Form: Submerged

**A** *Myriophyllum tuberculatum*

Distribution: Brazil & Peru
Reproduction: Cuttings
Hardiness: Medium
Form: Submerged

**B** *Najas guadalupensis*
*Copper Sensitive*

Distribution: Americas
Reproduction: Cuttings
Hardiness: Low
Form: Submerged

**A** *Najas indica*
*Copper Sensitive*

Distribution: Asia (Japan)
Reproduction: Cuttings
Hardiness: Low
Form: Submerged

**B** *Nesaea pedicellata*

Distribution: Tanzania, Mozambique
Reproduction: Seeds/Cuttings
Hardiness: Medium
Form: Emerged

**A** *Nesaea pedicellata*

Distribution: Tanzania, Mozambique
Reproduction: Seeds/Cuttings
Hardiness: Medium
Form: Submerged

**B** *Nesaea* sp. "Red"

Reproduction: Cuttings
Hardiness: Low
Form: Submerged

**C** *Nitella* spp.
*Copper Sensitive*

Reproduction: Cuttings
Hardiness: Low
Form: Submerged

**A** *Nuphar japonica*

Distribution: Southeast Asia
Reproduction: Seeds/Rhizome
Hardiness: Medium
Form: Submerged

**B** *Nuphar lutea* v. "Cape Fear"
Trade Name: **Cow Lily (Cape Fear)**

Distribution: Eastern U.S.A
Reproduction: Seeds/Rhizome
Hardiness: Low
Form: Submerged

**C** *Nuphar lutea* v. "Round Leaf"
Trade Name: **Cow Lily (Round Leaf)**

Distribution: North America
Reproduction: Seeds/Rhizome
Hardiness: Low
Form: Submerged

A Nymphaea daubenyana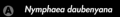
Reproduction: Rhizome/Adv. Shoot
Hardiness: Medium
Form: Submerged

B Nymphaea lotus v. "Green"
Trade Name: **Green Tiger Lotus**
Distribution: Madagascar & West Africa
Reproduction: Seeds/Bulbs
Hardiness: Medium
Form: Submerged

C Nymphaea lotus v. "Red"
Trade Name: **Red Tiger Lotus**
Distribution: Madagascar & West Africa
Reproduction: Seeds/Bulbs
Hardiness: Medium
Form: Submerged

*Nymphaea micrantha*

Distribution: West Africa
Reproduction: Seeds/Bulb/Adv. Shoot
Hardiness: Medium
Form: Submerged

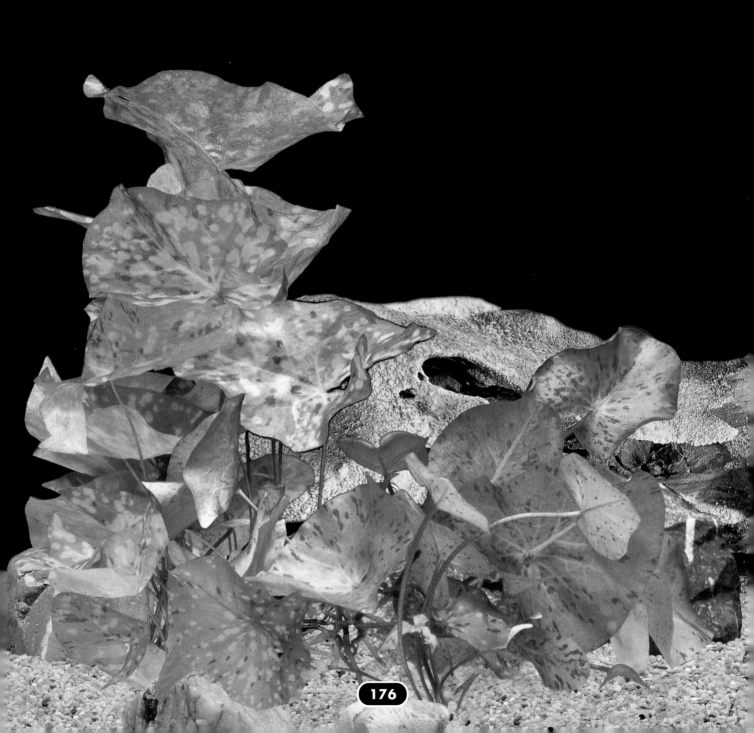

176

**A** *Nymphaea stellata*
Hardiness: Medium
Form: Submerged

**B** *Nymphaea stellata* v. "Versicolor"
Distribution: Sri Lanka
Reproduction: Seeds/Bulbs
Hardiness: Medium
Form: Submerged

**C** *Nymphoides aquatica*
Trade Name: **Banana Plant**
Distribution: Southeast U.S.A
Reproduction: Rhizome/Adv. Shoot
Hardiness: Medium
Form: Submerged

**A** *Copper Sensitive*

Hardiness: Low
Form: Submerged

**B** *Physostegia leptophylla*
Trade Name: **Florida Cryptocryne**

Distribution: Southeast U.S.A
Reproduction: Seeds/Rhizome
Hardiness: Medium
Form: Emerged

**A** *Polygonium hydropiperiodes*

Hardiness: Medium
Form: Emerged

**B** *Potamogeton crispus*
*Copper Sensitive*

Reproduction: Cuttings
Hardiness: Low
Form: Submerged

**Potamogeton guy.**
Copper Sensitive

Reproduction: Cuttings
Hardiness: Medium
Form: Submerged

**B**  **Potamogeton illinoinsis**
Copper Sensitive

Distribution: U.S.A
Reproduction: Runners/Cuttings
Hardiness: High
Form: Submerged

Form: Submerged

**Potamogeton sp. "Small"**
*Copper Sensitive*
Reproduction: Cuttings
Hardiness: Medium
Form: Submerged

181

 Trade Name: **Mermaid Weed**

Hardiness: Medium
Form: Emerged

**B** *Proserpinaca palustris*
Trade Name: **Mermaid Weed**

Distribution: Southeast U.S.A
Reproduction: Seeds/Cuttings
Hardiness: Medium
Form: Submerged

**A**

**B**

**A** *Proserpinaca pectinata*

Reproduction: Seeds, Cuttings
Hardiness: Low
Form: Emerged

**B** *Riccia* sp. "Fine Leaf"

Distribution: Southern U.S.A
Reproduction: Cuttings
Hardiness: Medium

**C** *Riccia fluitans*

Distribution: Worldwide
Reproduction: Cuttings
Hardiness: Medium

**Riccia fluitans**

Hardiness: Medium
Form: Submerged

**B** *Rorippa aquatica*

Distribution: United States
Reproduction: Seeds/Rhizome
Hardiness: Medium
Form: Emerged

**C** *Rorippa aquatica*

Distribution: United States
Reproduction: Seeds/Rhizome
Hardiness: Medium
Form: Submerged

Reproduction: Cuttings
Hardiness: Medium
Form: Submerged

(A) *Rotala macrandra*

Distribution: South India
Reproduction: Seeds/Cuttings
Hardiness: Medium
Form: Submerged

(B) *Rotala macrandra* v. "Narrow Leaf"

Distribution: Domestic
Reproduction: Cuttings
Hardiness: Medium
Form: Submerged

Ⓐ *Rotala rotundifolia*

Distribution: Southeast Asia
Reproduction: Seeds/Cuttings
Hardiness: High
Form: Emerged

Ⓑ *Rotala rotundifolia*

Distribution: Southeast Asia
Reproduction: Seeds/Cuttings
Hardiness: High
Form: Submerged

kolula wallichii

Hardiness: Medium
Form: Submerged

**B** *Sagittaria platyphylla*
Trade Name: **Broad Leaf Sagittaria**

Distribution: South U.S.A & Central America
Reproduction: Seeds/Runners
Hardiness: Medium
Form: Submerged

**C** *Sagittaria subulata*
Trade Name: **Narrow Leaf Sagittaria**

Distribution: South U.S.A & South America
Reproduction: Seeds/Runners
Hardiness: Medium
Form: Emerged

Trade Name: **Narrow Leaf Sagittaria**

Hardiness: Medium
Form: Submerged

**B** *Samolus valerandi*
Trade Name: **Water Rose**

Distribution: Worldwide
Reproduction: Seeds/Rhizome
Hardiness: Medium
Form: Emerged

Trade Name: **Water Orchid**

Hardiness: Medium
Form: Emerged

B *Shinnersia rivularis*
Trade Name: **Mexican Oakleaf**

Distribution: Texas & Mexico
Reproduction: Cuttings
Hardiness: Medium
Form: Emerged

Trade Name: **Variegated Mexican Oakleaf**

Hardiness: Medium
Form: Emerged

*Ultricularia* sp. "Jahore"
Trade Name: **Bladderwort**

Reproduction: Cuttings
Hardiness: Medium
Form: Submerged

Utricularia stellaris

Hardiness: Medium
Form: Submerged

**B** *Vallisneria americana*
Trade Name: **Jungle Val**

Distribution: North & Central America
Reproduction: Seeds/Runners
Hardiness: Medium
Form: Submerged

Trade Name: **Corkscrew Val**

Hardiness: Medium
Form: Submerged

*Vallisneria* **sp. "Asiatica"**
*Copper Sensitive*

Reproduction: Runners
Hardiness: Medium
Form: Submerged

Form: Submerged

*Vallisneria spiralis*
**B** Trade Name: **Italian Val**
*Copper Sensitive*

Distribution: Europe & Southwest Asia
Reproduction: Seeds/Runners
Hardiness: Medium
Form: Submerged

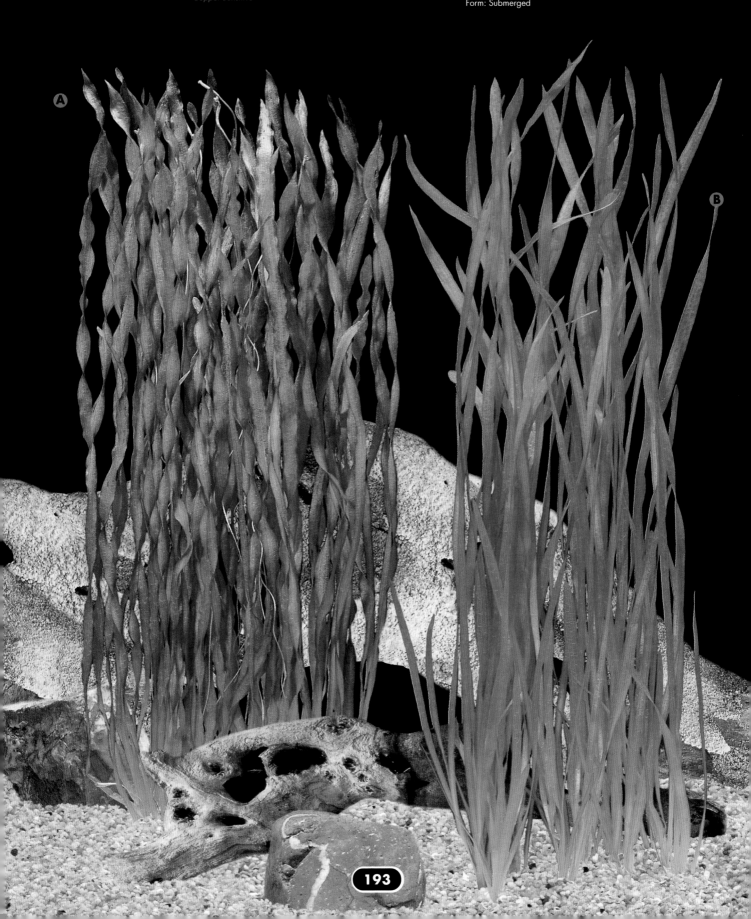

Trade Name: **Java Moss**

Hardiness: Medium
Form: Submerged

B *Zosterella dubia*
Copper Sensitive

Distribution: Americas
Reproduction: Cuttings
Hardiness: High
Form: Submerged

# Floating
# Plants

# Floating Plants ▪ Schwimmende Wasserpflanzen
# Plantes Aquatiques Flottantes ▪ Drijvende Waterplanten

As the name implies, these are true aquatic plants. However, I have put them in a separate section because they are not recommended for an aquarium. These plants float on the surface of the water and therefore are ideal for use in ponds. neutralize nitrogenous waste, they can often do more harm than good to your other aquarium plants. Since they float on the surface, they can block the light to the plants below.

If you still decide to use these plants in your aquarium, maintain them so that they do not cover too much of the water's surface.

Dies sind, wie Ihr Name schon besagt, echte Wasserpflanzen. Ich habe sie jedoch in einem separaten Abschnitt aufgeführt, weil sie für ein Aquarium nicht empfohlen werden.

Diese Pflanzen schwimmen auf der Wasseroberfläche und sind daher ideal für Teiche geeignet. Obwohl diese Pflanzen in einem Aquarium dazu dienen, stickstoffhaltige Abfälle zu neutralisieren, können sie anderen Aquariumpflanzen oft mehr schaden als nützen. Da sie auf der Oberfläche schwimmen, können sie das Licht für die sich darunter befindlichen Pflanzen blockieren. Wenn Sie diese Pflanzen trotzdem noch in Ihrem Aquarium verwenden wollen, achten Sie darauf, daß sie nicht zu viel Wasseroberfläche bedecken.

Comme leur nom l'indique, il s'agit de véritables plantes aquatiques. Toutefois, je les ai placées dans une autre partie, car elles ne sont pas recommandées dans un aquarium. Elles flottent à la surface de l'eau. Pour cette raison, elles sont idéales dans les bassins. Bien que ces plantes servent à neutraliser les déchets azotés, elles feront plus de dommages que de bien aux autres plantes de votre aquarium. En flottant à la surface, elles bloquent le passage de la lumière et empêchent les plantes plus basses de recevoir de l'énergie lumineuse. Si vous vous décidez tout de même d'en mettre dans votre aquarium, faites en sorte qu'elles ne couvrent jamais toute la surface de l'eau.

Zoals de naam het zegt zijn dit echte waterplanten. Ik behandel ze echter in een afzonderlijke paragraaf omdat ze niet aan te bevelen zijn voor een aquarium. Deze planten drijven op het wateroppervlak en zijn daarom eerder te gebruiken in open aquaria of vijvers. Nochthans gebruikt in een aquarium om stikstofhoudend afval te neutraliseren, kunnen deze planten soms meer kwaad dan goed doen aan de andere aquariumplanten. Aangezien ze aan de oppervlakte drijven kunnen ze het licht belemmeren voor de andere planten. Wanneer u echter toch kiest voor dergelijke planten, beperk ze, zodat ze niet teveel van het wateroppervlak bedekken

**Altenanthera piloxeroides**

**Aponogeton distachyos**

**Azolla caroliniana**

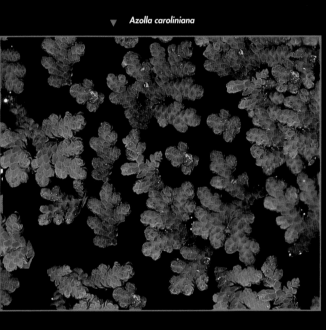

**Ceratopteris pteridoides**

**Eichhornia crassipes**

**Hydroeleys nymphoides**

*Lemna minor*

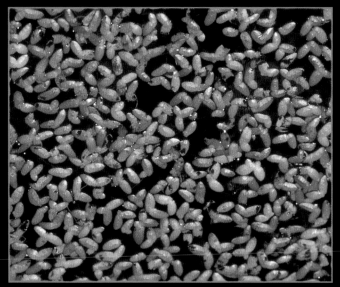

*Limnobium spongia*

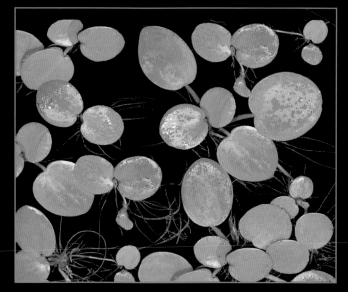

*Ludwigia sedioides*

*Myriophyllum aquaticum* (Floating)

*Pistia* sp. "Rosette"

*Pistia stratiotes*

▼ *Salvinia rotundifolia*

▼ *Spirodela polyrhiza*

▼ *Utricularia gibba*

▼ *Wolffia* spp.

# Terrarium Plants

## Bog Plants ▪ Terrestrial Plants

# Bog Plants ▪ Moospflanzen
# Les Plantes de Marais ▪ Moerasplanten

This section shows which plants to avoid in your aquarium. Photos and names are given but no extra data is included because I don't feel that you should even consider using these in an aquarium.

With so many beautiful true aquarium plants to choose from, why would anyone want to put any of these plants in his or her tank? This section is divided into Bog Plants and Terrestrial Plants.

**Bog plants** are suited for wet environments; their root systems are capable of being moist or subm-erged permanently, as long as their leaves are above water. If they are totally submerged, they will die.

In diesem Abschnitt erfahren Sie, welche Pflanzen Sie in Ihrem Aquarium vermeiden sollten. Er enthält Fotos und Namen, aber keine Extradaten, weil ich der Meinung bin, Sie sollten die Verwendung dieser Pflanzen in einem Aquarium gar nicht erst in Erwägung ziehen. Warum sollte man eine dieser Pflanzen in sein Aquarium setzen, wenn es so viele echte Aquariumpflanzen gibt, unter denen man auswählen kann? Dieser Abschnitt ist in Moospflanzen und Erdpflanzen unterteilt.

**Moospflanzen** sind für nasse Umgebungen geeignet, ihre Wurzelsysteme können entweder feucht oder permanent unter Wasser sein, so lange sich ihre Blätter über Wasser befinden. Wenn sie vollständig unter Wasser sind, werden sie sterben.

Cette partie vous indique quelles plantes il vous faut éviter de placer dans l'aquarium. On vous en donne les photos et les noms, mais aucunes autres données, car j'estime qu'on ne doit même pas penser les rentrer dans l'aquarium. Le choix est déja tellement large dans la famille des plantes aquatiques. Pourquoi devrait-on alors employer des plantes non aquatiques? Cette partie parle des plantes de marais et des plantes terrestres.

**Les plantes de marais** conviennent dans des biotopes humides. Leur système de racines peut être humidifié ou submergé constamment, tant que leurs feuilles ne sont pas plongées dans l'eau. Si elles sont totalement plongées dans l'eau, elles meurent.

Deze paragraaf leert welke planten u best niet gebruikt in uw aquarium. Er worden foto's en namen gegeven maar verder geen informatie omdat ik niet de idee heb dat u er ook maar even aan denkt die in een aquarium te gebruiken.

Waarom zou iemand dergelijke planten in een aquarium plaatsen wanneer er zoveel mooie, echte aquariumplanten beschikbaar zijn? Terrariumplanten zijn deels moeras-, deels vaste planten.

**Moerasplanten** zijn geschikt voor een natte omgeving: de worteling is van die aard dat die in staat is te gedijen ofwel op een vochtige plaats ofwel onder water, zolang de bladeren maar boven water blijven. Als je de plant volledig onder water zet zal ze sterven.

▼ *Acorus gramineus v. "Variegated"*          ▼ *Acrostichum aureum*

▼ *Adantum raddianum*          ▼ *Altenanthera philoxeroides*

▼ *Alternanthera ficoidea* v. "Bronze"

▼ *Alternanthera ficoidea* v. "Cherry Stem"

▼ *Alternanthera ficoidea* v. "Green"

▼ *Alternanthera sessilis*

▼ *Aponogeton distachyos*

▼ *Chlorophytum bichettii*

Cyperus helferi

Gendarussa vulgaris

Houttuynia cordata

Houttuynia cordata v. "Variegated"

Marsilea crenata

Marsilea quadrifolia

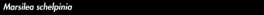

*Marsilea schelpinia*

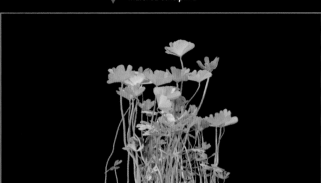

*Oenanthe javanicum* v. "Flamingo"

*Ophipogon japonica*

*Ophipogon japonica* v. "Kyoto Dwarf"

*Ophipogon japonica* v. "Silvermist"

*Pteris vittata*

205

▼ *Spathiphyllum tasson*

▼ *Trichomanes javanicum*

▼ *Viola esculenta*

▼ *Zephranthes candida*

# Terrestrial Plants ▪ Erdpflanzen
# Les Plantes Terrestres ▪ Vaste Planten

**Terrestrial plants** need an even drier environment than bog plants do. Their roots cannot sit in the water for an extended period of time without developing root rot. They may be submerged for an (extremely) limited time, but this isn't recommended.

**Erdpflanzen** benötigen eine trockenere Umgebung als Moospflanzen. Ihre Wurzeln können nicht längere Zeit im Wasser stecken, ohne daß sie Wurzelfäule entwickeln. Sie können sich eine (extrem) beschränkte Zeit unter Wasser befinden, aber dies wird nicht empfohlen.

**Les plantes terrestres** ont besoin d'un substrat plus sec que les plantes de marais. Leurs racines ne peuvent rester de façon permanente dans l'eau. On peut les laisser dans l'eau pendant une petite période, mais cela n'est pas recommandé.

●

**Vaste planten** hebben een drogere omgeving nodig dan moerasplanten. Hun wortels kunnen niet voor een lange periode onder water vertoeven. Ze mogen wel onder water gezet worden voor een (zeer) korte duur maar dat is niet aan te bevelen.

**Aglaonema comutatum**

**Chamaedorea elegans**

**Cordyllne terminalis**

**Dracaena borenquensis**

**Dracaena compacta**

**Dracaena godseffianna**

*Dracaena marginatus* v. "Colorama"

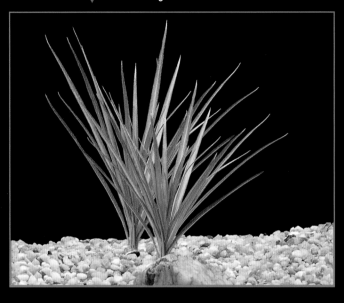

*Dracaena sanderiana*

*Dracaena thaliodes*

*Hemigraphis exotica*

*Hemigraphis repanda*

*Liriope muscani* v. "Variegated"

Pilea cadierei

Syngonium podophyllum v. "Regina Red"

Syngonium podophyllum v. "White Butterfly"

# Index

*Notes:*

• *All plant scientific and trade names are included in this index.*

• *All plants are marked as **submerged** with an **(s)**, **emerged** with an **(e)**, **floating** with an **(f)**, or **terrarium** with a **(t)**.*

# Index

# Index

# Index

# Index

# Literature & Colofon

*Literature:*

KASSELMANN, Christel. *Aquarienpflanzen*
DATZ-Atlanten; Stuttgard, Germany, 1995 (1st Ed.)

*Colofon:*

This book was typeset on a Apple Macintosh 9500/132 running *Adobe PageMaker 6.5*. The icons were produced in *Adobe Illustrator 7.0* for Macintosh.

Pages containing Chinese and Japanese text were typeset using *Adobe PageMaker 6.5Chinese*.

Roman fonts used are ITC Eras Demi, the Adobe Garamond family, and the ITC Futura family.

Japanese type used were members of the Adobe Hesei Kaku Gothic family and the Hesei Min family. Chinese fonts used were DF Hei Bold, and DF Kai Shu Medium.